T0084775

The Chicago Guide to **Copyediting Fiction**

Chicago Guides
to *Writing*, Editing,
and Publishing

The Chicago Guide to

Copyediting Fiction

AMY J. SCHNEIDER

THE UNIVERSITY OF CHICAGO PRESS

Chicago and London

The University of Chicago Press, Chicago 60637
The University of Chicago Press, Ltd., London

Published 2023

Printed in the United States of America

32 31 30 29 28 27 26 25 24 23   1 2 3 4 5

ISBN-13: 978-0-226-82304-1 (cloth)
ISBN-13: 978-0-226-76737-6 (paper)
ISBN-13: 978-0-226-82302-7 (e-book)
DOI: https://doi.org/10.7208/chicago/9780226823027.001.0001

Library of Congress Cataloging-in-Publication Data

Names: Schneider, Amy J., author.
Title: The Chicago guide to copyediting fiction / Amy J. Schneider.
Other titles: Chicago guides to writing, editing, and publishing.
Description: Chicago ; London : The University of Chicago Press, 2023. |
    Series: Chicago guides to writing, editing, and publishing | Includes
    bibliographical references and index.
Identifiers: LCCN 2022022493 | ISBN 9780226823041 (cloth) |
    ISBN 9780226767376 (paperback) | ISBN 9780226823027 (ebook)
Subjects: LCSH: Fiction—Editing | Copy editing. | Editing.
Classification: LCC PN162 .S227 2023 | DDC 135/.45—dc23/eng/20220930
LC record available at https://lccn.loc.gov/2022022493

♾ This paper meets the requirements of ANSI/NISO Z39.48-1992
(Permanence of Paper).

Contents

Introduction

Congratulations! You've landed your first fiction copyediting project. It's a novel in a genre you read for pleasure, and you expect that this job will be fun and easy. You open the file and start reading. It's an intriguing story, and you quickly find yourself catching typos. This is great! But after a few chapters, you start to notice some odd things. In many places the editorial style does not conform to the style manual you are most familiar with. There are three different characters named Kevin, and you think two of them might be the same person, but you're not sure. Tara lives in a second-floor apartment, but also walks out her front door onto the street. Chris went to school on Friday . . . and then again the next day . . . and the next day too. You notice that characters don't speak in the formal, "correct" English you learned in high school—should you fix it? There are comma splices and sentence fragments and made-up words that aren't in the dictionary. The description of one character feels like an offensive stereotype; is that okay if it's fictional? Is this dialogue punctuated correctly? Can the author really use *fumbled* as a synonym for *said*? Could Jamaal have broken his Game Boy when he was seven years old, if he's forty-five now? Can you even mention a Game Boy in a novel, or do you have to get permission? The more things you notice, the more you realize that perhaps copyediting fiction isn't as simple or straightforward as you thought.

I've been copyediting fiction (as well as nonfiction) since the beginning of my career. When I was a wee baby copyeditor in 1995, I didn't know about the conventional wisdom that be-

fore you jump into freelancing, you should spend several years working in-house for a publisher or another publication department and
get some on-the-job training. But jump in I did, and part of my self-
training was reading what may have been the only book about copyediting at that time: Karen Judd's *Copyediting: A Practical Guide*. I
was so excited to read in her opening pages about the sorts of things
a born copyeditor would catch. That's me! And that's me! And that's
also me! And so a copyeditor[1] was born.

Although Judd's book has become technologically outdated, the
editorial concepts still apply. But like many copyediting resources,
it spends little time on fiction. I built my approach to copyediting
fiction based on about a page and a half of discussion from Judd's
book. I've expanded it in the years since then, both as a result of my
increasing experience and to match the progression of copyediting
from paper to the screen.

This book reflects what I've learned about the art of copyediting
fiction, on my own and from others. The concept grew out of many
conversations with fellow editors who, upon learning that I copyedit
fiction, wanted to know more about my process. As you will discover
in these pages, there is no standard way to copyedit a work of fiction.
There are nearly as many styles as there are manuscripts, authors,
and publishers. And so this book is *not* a style manual or a grammar
text, laying out rules to be imposed on every manuscript. Rather, it
is intended as food for thought, a road map for helping each author,
character, and manuscript tell their own story in their own voice and
their own style, clearly and consistently.

The Chicago Guide to Copyediting Fiction assumes that the reader
has a basic familiarity with the process of copyediting and has several years of copyediting experience. It is not a guide to Copyediting
101 but rather a guide to Copyediting Fiction 101. If you are new to
copyediting, I recommend that you investigate certificate programs,
courses, and other training offered by universities and professional
organizations, such as those mentioned in the Recommended Re-

---

1. Copyeditors disagree on whether the term for their profession is one word
or two. I follow Judd's philosophy that "a copyeditor does not edit copy; a copyeditor *copyedits* copy" (2nd ed., p. 1).

sources at the back of this book, to learn the basics. Many of these programs are available as online learning. Amy Einsohn and Marilyn Schwartz's *The Copyeditor's Handbook* and its accompanying workbook offer a comprehensive resource and reference. Katharine O'Moore-Klopf's Copyeditors' Knowledge Base (kokedit.com/ckb .php) is chock-full of annotated links to resources on training as well as running an editorial business, editorial tools, networking, marketing, and more.

I write from the perspective of having worked only with traditional publishers rather than independent ("indie"), or self-published, authors. Manuscripts that come from publishers have already been accepted for publication and may have undergone developmental and line editing; the plot and mechanics are already well polished, and the publisher and the copyeditor should largely agree about what copyediting entails. If you are working with indie authors, you may also offer more big-picture types of editing, such as developmental editing, either separately or in a bundle of services along with copyediting. (And you will often need to have in-depth conversations with indie authors about their expectations for each level of editing; your definitions and their definitions will often differ, so agreeing on parameters will save everyone time and frustration.) Those earlier levels of editing are a separate topic well covered by other resources, although we will discuss how to notify the author at the copyediting stage if certain issues have fallen through the cracks. The Writers and Editors website and blog (writersandeditors.com), like the Copyeditors' Knowledge Base, has lots of links to resources that will be useful to editors who offer services to indie authors such as formatting for ebooks or for submission to agents, particularly on the "For Editors and Publishing Professionals" page (writersandeditors.com/for_editors_57430.htm).

This book primarily addresses copyediting novels,[2] novellas, and short stories. Although many of the principles discussed may apply

2. As long as we are talking about novels, let me remind everyone that "fiction novel" is redundant. Yes, I know about Truman Capote's nonfiction novel *In Cold Blood*. That genre is a rare exception; 99.9999 percent of people who write or say "fiction novel" are talking about a plain-vanilla novel, which by default and unless otherwise defined is understood to mean a work of fiction.

to copyediting works such as graphic novels, screenplays, and poetry, those are different specialties in which I have not worked, and thus they are a topic for a different book.

The principles discussed here can be applied to either hard-copy (paper) or electronic copyediting; however, I wrote it with electronic copyediting in mind, as that is the most common method of copyediting manuscripts in US book publishing. While Microsoft Word is the industry-standard software, copyediting is also done in other formats such as PDF and Google Docs, especially for indie authors. Examples in this book refer to Microsoft Word 2019 for Windows. Specific details or instructions for other versions may vary, so you should consult resources for your particular platform or software version. The use of efficiency tools such as editing-specific Word plug-ins and macros is a separate topic; I mention them briefly here and there and provide some useful resources at the back of the book. Adrienne Montgomerie demonstrates basic PDF markup on her website (http://scieditor.ca), and Karin Horler's *Google Docs for Editors* is an excellent guide to using Google Docs to collaborate with authors.

Most fiction copyediting in the United States is done by freelance editors working for publishers and indie authors, rather than by in-house employees. I've been freelancing full-time my entire career, so that is the perspective I bring to this book; however, most of the information on copyediting within these pages applies equally well if you are working in-house for an employer. See Katharine O'Moore-Klopf's Copyeditors' Knowledge Base and Writers and Editors (discussed earlier; these are also listed in the Recommended Resources) for information on business topics such as how to find clients, set rates, provide estimates, negotiate scope of work, create contracts or letters of agreement, and so on. Erin Brenner of Right Touch Editing (righttouchediting.com) also writes extensively on business topics for freelance editors.

The primary style guide[3] for book publishing in the United States

---

3. I use the terms *style guide* and *style manual* somewhat interchangeably; generally, *style manual* connotes a standard style reference such as *The Chicago Manual of Style* (*CMOS*) or *New Hart's Rules*, whereas *style guide* refers to an internal document used by a publisher, corporation, or journal. However, in

is *The Chicago Manual of Style* (*CMOS*), available in print or online at chicagomanualofstyle.org, and I refer to it often here. *CMOS* is devoted primarily to nonfiction; however, much of its guidance can be applied to fiction—with the caveat that fiction frequently deviates from *CMOS* and other traditional "rules." If your primary style guide is a different one—for example, if you are working with Australian, British, or Canadian English—refer to the comparable sections in that style guide. (See the sidebar titled "Publisher House Style" in chapter 2 and the Recommended Resources at the back of this book.)

If you are a fiction author, you may also find this book useful as a peek into what kinds of things your copyeditor will be watching for, as well as a guide to self-editing before submission. A good copyeditor will do their[4] best to preserve your voice; any information you provide, such as your personal style preferences and any backstory or character profiles you may have developed, will help smooth the process.

Part I of this book provides an overview of the fiction copyeditor's approach to the manuscript, both philosophical and practical. Part II covers the particulars of building a fiction style sheet: recording general style, characters, places, and timeline. Part III covers issues specific to fiction: grammar and usage, handling dialogue, and blending fact and fiction. Several sidebars discuss peripheral topics such as zombie rules, technical tools, and narrative distance. Appendixes cover some additional material: style sheet templates, file management, and multiple monitors. A brief glossary and a list of recommended resources appear at the end of the book. (Glossary terms appear in italics near where they are defined and discussed.)

Now that the housekeeping is out of the way, it's time to get into the good stuff!

---

general conversation, editors are just as likely to ask "What style guide are you using?" And if a client's in-house style reference is 125 pages long, we might as well call it a manual.

4. Throughout this book, I embrace the growing acceptance of the use of singular *they*, both as a gender-neutral pronoun to avoid awkward and unnecessary rewrites ("he or she" and the like) and to be inclusive of nonbinary people. See Gael Spivak's post on singular *they* on the Government of Canada's *Our Languages* blog, which includes a link to a list of more than forty articles supporting its use.

Part I

The Process of Copyediting Fiction

Fiction differs from nonfiction in that it is not a structured presentation of facts and ideas but a product of the author's imagination, a portrait painted in words. Thus the copyeditor must lay aside many of the editorial conventions they learned from standard guides and instruction in the profession that apply to nonfiction, understand when to relax the "rules," and look at how each edit serves the story and ensures that it makes sense, whether it takes place in the real world or an invented one. The copyeditor considers the requirements of the genre, the author, the readers, and the publisher to polish the manuscript and make it shine.

Part I of this book discusses both this mindset that the fiction copyeditor must cultivate and the workflow involved in copyediting fiction: manuscript intake and cleanup, creating and organizing style sheets for various types of manuscripts, and completing multiple copyediting passes before returning the manuscript to the client. And so we begin.

1

The Fiction Copyeditor's Mindset

Authors are artists, especially in fiction; the page is their canvas, words are their paints, and voice and style are their brushes. Is the narration straightforward or more evocative? How do the characters speak? What point(s) of view has the author chosen? These differ for every manuscript, and the best fiction copyeditors are flexible enough to approach each one with a fresh and attentive eye.

When I started freelancing, my bread and butter was copyediting college textbooks. Very formulaic, strong adherence to rules and style guides and real-world facts. So when I started copyediting fiction, I worried about interfering with the story or upsetting the author. These are legitimate concerns. But copyediting fiction just means wearing a different hat. Instead of keeping the text 100 percent in line with the real world, a fiction copyeditor ensures that the story is internally consistent within its *own* world, whether real or fictional. This means checking both real-world facts (are there mountains in Ohio?) and fictional ones (which colors of magic stones are sentient and which are not?). Errors in either case may interfere with the reader's enjoyment of the story; however, authors sometimes deliberately fictionalize locations and other facts for various reasons.

Today, when I mention that I spend much of my professional life copyediting fiction, colleagues (especially those who have edited only nonfiction) and laypeople alike are often fascinated. *Wow, so you earn your living by reading romances and thrillers? Neat!* Well, as with all editing, there's a *bit* more

Words of Wisdom

Three important mottoes for any copyeditor, and especially for fiction copyeditors, are "It's not my book," "Is this how people talk?" and "If it ain't broke, don't fix it." Chapters 7 and 8 discuss these topics in more detail.

"It's not my book"

Respect the author's choices. There are all kinds of grammar and all kinds of punctuation and all kinds of styles. You may be called on to edit in a variety of ways, some of which may go against your personal preference in your own writing. And that's okay.

"Is this how people talk?"

Don't change something just because it's informal, or "wrong," or not the word you would choose—especially in dialogue or first-person narration. Not everyone speaks the same way you do, and people don't edit spontaneous speech to be "perfect." I recently learned a lot about Irish dialect while copyediting a novel by an Irish author featuring Irish characters, by looking up words, phrases, and constructions that were unfamiliar to me and adding them to the style sheet with a definition or explanation. Let characters and narrators have their own voice, especially when it is an expression of their culture or personal history.

"If it ain't broke, don't fix it"

Don't rewrite just to avoid a tricky point of grammar or punctuation. That word that's unfamiliar to you may be perfectly legit; you may need to brush up on your grammar or punctuation skills to be able to edit a passage without changing the author's intent. At the same time, don't fix it if it's intentionally broke. Overly pedantic copyeditors are the bane of the fiction author's world. Don't be one.

to it than just reading. The fiction copyeditor must remember not to get so caught up in the story that they forget to edit judiciously. This book will help you focus on the mechanical details while keeping the story in line.

What fiction copyediting is not

Copyediting fiction requires the copyeditor to set aside many of the conventions of editing nonfiction (though not all) that are featured in standard training resources and to develop a different mindset that enables them to do justice to each manuscript. Part of that mindset consists of recognizing what a fiction copyeditor should *not* be doing. Let's look at some examples.

This is not your chance to pretend you are the author. I took my first fiction copyediting test very early in my career, on a whim. And when I learned that I had passed with flying colors, I actually protested to the managing editor who was hiring me: "I don't know anything about writing fiction! How can I possibly copyedit it?" She laughed and assured me that she preferred to hire copyeditors who won't try to (re)write the author's book for them. If you are an aspiring or actual novelist, this is not the time to try to take over the telling of the story or to critique the work. Your job is mechanical only. You may set your writer's or critic's hat off to the side and glance at it from time to time as you copyedit, but do not even think about putting it on. A common saying among editors is "It's not my book" (see the sidebar titled "Words of Wisdom"), and this also applies when you are copyediting fiction. When you are copyediting for a publisher, it's too late to worry about whether a character is properly developed, pacing is appropriate, and so on. Those decisions have already been made and approved during previous discussions between the author and the acquisitions or developmental editor, and unless there's a huge plot hole, your job is to focus on the mechanics of copyediting. If you are editing for an indie author, your scope may be wider—for example, if you are offering a bundle of developmental editing and copyediting—but that would need to be specified in your agreement with the author. If your role is strictly copyediting and that is what the author is paying you for, stick to the agreement.

This is not the place to apply your own moral code. You may encounter naughty words, unpleasant people and actions, blood and gore, blasphemy, and sex scenes. Your job is to copyedit the narration and dialogue in all its unsavory glory. For personal reasons, you may choose not to accept projects in genres such as erotica or violent military or paranormal thrillers—but once you do, you're duty bound to edit the text respectfully and keep it true to itself. (Is that term for a sexual act one word or two? Decide and put it on the style sheet. Not every style sheet is rated PG.) If you feel that you cannot give the manuscript your full professional attention, let the publisher or author know immediately that you are not the right copyeditor for the job so they can find one who is.

This is not the time to apply your grammar hammer. In fiction, grammar, punctuation, syntax, style, and the like are much more fluid. Fiction authors often use (or invent) words to paint a picture, create a mood, wax poetic. Characters may or may not speak formal English, whether in dialogue or in first-person narration. If you are a stickler for language "perfection," you must retrain your brain when copyediting fiction. Mind, it's not a free-for-all, and when copyediting for a publisher, you need to balance house style against the author's voice, but you must also be aware of when it's okay (or necessary) to break the rules.

Breaking the rules?

Yep, I said breaking the rules. (And knowing which rules aren't really rules; see the sidebar titled "The First Thing We Do, Let's Kill All the Zombies.") Fiction often dances to its own beat. Here are some common examples; I discuss these and more in greater detail in later chapters.

- Comma splices, sentence fragments, and repetition are common techniques for creating a particular pace, a character's voice, tension, a casual feel.
- Characters have their own voices: they speak in accents and dialects, they have quirky mannerisms, they have different levels of education, they're tired, they stutter, they interrupt themselves and each other, they use slang and vulgar words,

and so on. Dialogue is usually much more free-form than narration. That said, however . . .

- First-person narration often uses the same level of colloquial language that's found in dialogue.
- By the same token, written notes, text messages, emails, and other casual communication are often as free-form as spoken dialogue.

Let characters have their natural voice: level of formality, use of dialect, invented vocabulary, and so on. Stet casual style unless there's a good reason to change it, such as awkward phrasing, garden-path sentences (see chapter 7), or other problems that force readers to

The First Thing We Do, Let's Kill All the Zombies

Learn to let go of *zombie rules*, those outdated and sometimes incorrect grammar or usage rules that few people observe: People can say *decimate* when they mean "destroy," not the older definition of "to reduce by one-tenth." *Over* can be used to mean "more than" and not just "physically above." *Between* can be used to compare more than two items. It's okay to split an infinitive and end a sentence with a preposition and use *impact* as a verb. Erin Brenner of Right Touch Editing has written an excellent blog post series on zombie rules that covers these and other common examples of "rules" that aren't rules (righttouchediting.com/tag/zombie-rules/).

Many editors and other language nerds are aware of these "rules," but only they ("and not all of them," she said, raising her hand) can tell you the difference between *compare to* and *compare with*. A prime example is the *who/whom* distinction, which is rapidly losing ground in all but the most formal writing. Language evolves and editing is descriptive. So embrace change and free your mind.

work to figure out the meaning. Edit for clarity, but don't edit the life out of the story.

Supporting suspension of disbelief

In fiction, the copyeditor is like the continuity supervisor on a movie set. Everything must fit the logic of the world the author has created, whether it's in twelfth-century Pakistan or Sector 9 of the T'Yara system. Fact-checking in fiction goes beyond real-world facts to cover any fact in that fictional setting that could be contradicted elsewhere. Readers notice even the most obscure errors and discrepancies, whether from general life experience or from specialized knowledge; the copyeditor's job is to ferret out these errors and help the author eradicate them, so they don't pull readers out of the story.

ENSURING INTERNAL CONSISTENCY

The manuscript serves as its own reference source (and if it's part of a series, the previous books provide additional canon). Its reality may be based on real-world people, places, objects, situations, history, languages, technology, species, and physics; a completely made-up world set in an imaginary place with invented or fictionalized versions of these; or a mix of both. The copyeditor creates a *style sheet* that organizes all of the "facts" (real and fictional) and style choices (the combination of book style, author style, and publisher house style) of that particular manuscript, providing a guide with which to ensure internal consistency. See part II for details on building a fiction style sheet.

CALLING OUT POTENTIAL PROBLEMS

The author may have made deliberate choices that nevertheless may give readers pause; other consistency issues crop up as a result of revisions made before the copyediting stage. Your job is to call possible problems to the author's attention for their review. For example, should recalled dialogue or repeated text match exactly? If it doesn't, will readers think it's an error? Should real street names or directions be accurate? Will readers familiar with that city be pulled out of the story if they aren't? Was an unusual but possible word choice intentional? If so, will readers trip on it? Some issues are particu-

lar to or more prevalent in fiction as opposed to nonfiction. A few
examples:

- Unintentional alliteration, assonance, consonance, and
  rhyming can distract readers, who often experience the text
  with their ears as well as their eyes (whether in their own
  heads while reading silently, while reading aloud, or while
  listening to an audiobook or screen reader). Distractions
  include consecutive sentences or phrases that end with the
  same word or syllable, as well as possibly unintentional
  repetition of similar words or sounds. (See chapter 7 to learn
  how to tune in to unintended "sound effects.")
- Dialogue tags (*she said*) are easily over- or underused. They
  must appear frequently enough to identify who is speaking but
  not so often as to be intrusive; the author may use only *said*
  and *asked* or sprinkle in more descriptive tags like *muttered*
  and *whined*. (See chapter 8 for an extensive discussion of
  dialogue tags.)
- Anachronisms in narration and dialogue appear in historical
  fiction and in modern settings. Was it possible to send a
  text message from a mobile phone in 1993? In a novel set in
  ancient Mesopotamia, will it jar the reader if a young boy
  uses modern teenage slang? Was the *Empress of Scotland* in
  service as a passenger liner in 1913? At the same time, authors
  sometimes deliberately fictionalize real characters, places, or
  events for creative reasons, which are often explained in an
  afterword. (See chapter 9 for further discussion of ferreting
  out anachronisms.)

One school of thought suggests that the author's creative choices
are sacred and that the author has the final say, even if such choices
seem "wrong." That's true; it's the author's book, not the copyeditor's. But part of the copyeditor's due diligence is letting the author
know about potential problems, explaining why they might make
readers stumble or lose interest, and offering possible alternatives.
And in my experience, many authors appreciate this attention to
detail. One author whose previous novels I had copyedited told
the publisher that as they were writing their next book, they were

about to let a minor inconsistent detail slide—but then realized that I would notice and call it out, so they fixed it right away instead. Everyone wins!

ADVOCATING FOR THE READER

When you copyedit fiction, you are not only helping the author get their work into the best possible shape but also helping the reader remain immersed in the story. Have you ever tossed a novel aside because of a detail that defied logic, or left a plot hole, or was factually wrong? Perhaps a character had an outlandish name that made no sense or looked like a typo. Perhaps you have specialized knowledge about a subject (a profession or hobby, a location and its culture, a historical era) and the story has it wrong. Perhaps an important real event never happens in the story, without explanation. Perhaps you couldn't figure out who was talking in long stretches of dialogue. Such infelicities are distracting and disappointing and may put off a reader from finishing the book or even reading that author or that genre altogether. A good copyeditor helps the author remember the needs of the reader.

Developing a deeper understanding

As you copyedit more and more manuscripts and build relationships with authors and publishers, much of your understanding of the following topics will become second nature; you'll become familiar with the genres you specialize in, get to know repeat authors and their style, understand what their readers are looking for, and develop relationships with publishers and learn their expectations. Let's look at some of the particulars.

GENRE

Different genres and their subgenres have different sets of conventions that readers expect and are familiar with. A savvy copyeditor is familiar with these conventions as well. Here are a few examples:

- Fantasy: invented worlds, special terms, lots of backstory, creative naming conventions

- Literary fiction: evocative imagery, philosophical themes, character focus, symbolism and allegory
- Military: lots of technical information, profanity, violence
- Mystery: a crime, suspense, foreshadowing, a resolution
- Romance: formulaic plot arc, possible sex scenes, a happily-ever-after
- Science fiction: invented worlds and languages, alien civilizations, space travel, time travel
- Thrillers: a sneaky antagonist, false clues, suspense and tension
- YA (young adult): slang, informal grammar, current pop culture references, characters who were born in an online world

How can you develop your understanding of genres? By reading them. This can be the reading that you do as part of your copyediting, but it can also be your pleasure reading. Seek out bestselling authors. Ask for recommendations. Read reviews. Join online forums for fans of genre fiction at book-related websites such as Goodreads and on social media in general. And did I mention reading?

AUTHOR

Take a few minutes to get to know the author a little bit before starting to copyedit a manuscript. (This is good advice for any copyediting project, but especially for fiction.) When you work directly for an indie author, this is a natural part of the relationship-building process; you might arrange a conversation about their experience and their goals or send them a detailed questionnaire. However, when you work for a publisher as a freelance copyeditor, you are seldom in direct contact with the author; you copyedit the manuscript, write your queries (see chapter 2), and send everything back to the publisher. The End. Some publishers have the copyeditor do the cleanup (also discussed in chapter 2), in which case you'll be able to see the author's responses to your edits and queries. But except in special cases, you can't contact the author directly; many publishers do not even give the author the copyeditor's name, unless the author wishes to thank them in the acknowledgments or requests them for their next book. So if you copyedit for publishers, your communication with the author is likely to be one-way.[1]

If you're not already familiar with the author, visit their page on the publisher's website, their own website and social media pages, and their reviews on sites like Amazon and Goodreads. Are they a first-time author or a regular on the bestseller lists? Are they known for a particular character, series, or genre? Do they have specialized knowledge or life experience? Is their style conventional or quirky? Find a photo if you can, to keep an image of them in the back of your mind as you edit. Investing this small amount of time helps you connect with the author indirectly and remember the person behind the manuscript and what they are trying to accomplish. (See also the section titled "Conscious language" in chapter 7 for more reasons to learn about the author before accepting a project or starting an edit.)

READERS

The flip side of learning about the author is learning about their audience. Popular, established authors have a fan base who have expectations about upcoming books, whether they are part of a series or stand-alone titles. Fans of a particular genre expect to encounter its usual elements; fans of a series are familiar with the characters, terminology, and backstory of that world, so subsequent books won't need as much explanation as the first book in a series or solo books. Online fan groups, for a genre or a particular author, are an excellent resource.

A work of fiction is meant to provide an escape, a mini-vacation into a different place or time or world. The style, voice, mechanics, plotting, pacing, and all the other details must uphold that effect in order to serve the reader. The copyeditor must not only pay attention

---

1. In a rare exception, an author once asked the publisher for permission to email me directly after the copyedit; I had written some extensive queries offering information and suggesting solutions regarding a plot in the story involving a subject about which I have specialized knowledge, and the author had additional questions. We had a lovely conversation, and the author was so grateful for my help that she sent me an inscribed copy of the book and a small gift. So you never know!

to these aspects but also see the story as the reader will see it and ensure that everything makes sense.

PUBLISHER

If your client is a publisher, you must blend their house style with the author's writing style (see the sidebar titled "Publisher House Style"). Ideally the publisher will guide you on where to conform to house style and where to let the author's style prevail. They may ask you to deal with problem areas such as repetition or loose ends in the plot. The publisher also is your intermediary when you do not have direct contact with the author; for example, they may tell you that the author is sensitive to being edited and to copyedit with a very light hand and extra-gentle queries (see chapter 2), or that the author would appreciate extra fact-checking on the location where the story is set. Publishers usually have well-defined production schedules, so you must communicate with your project manager as soon as possible if you think you can't meet a deadline, if the manuscript needs more work than expected, or if you spot a major problem that needs the author's attention before you can proceed.

Publisher House Style

Most book publishers in the United States follow *CMOS* as their primary style guide, but many also have a *house style* that lays out their own preferences, some of which may conform to *CMOS* and some of which may not. House style may be as simple as a few stated preferences that the project manager conveys when transmitting the manuscript to you, or it may be a multipage document that is regularly updated. Most of the time publishers want you to follow *CMOS* unless their house style overrides it. When you copyedit for a publisher, always ask if they have a house style guide and save a copy of it for future reference.

I like to think of the job of copyediting fiction as sanding off the rough edges. The author has done the design and construction; I'm just smoothing and polishing, maybe pounding in a nail that sticks out here or there, maybe applying a little putty where something had to be taken apart and redone. If I've done my job correctly, my work is invisible—but it shows off the author's creation to its best advantage.

2

The Fiction Copyeditor's Workflow

After you've accepted the project, it may seem tempting to just open the manuscript and start reading. But you'll need to set up your process and workspace first. This includes looking over the manuscript file for any technical or formatting issues, starting a style sheet, and reviewing the style to be used and any notes from the client. This chapter closes with a discussion of how to write tactful and effective queries and a brief overview of proofreading fiction.

Receiving the manuscript

If your manuscript has come from a traditional publisher, it has already been accepted for publication and may have undergone developmental and substantive editing. (See *CMOS*, chapter 2, for a discussion of these "big-picture" levels of editing.) The publisher may also have run a typographic cleanup routine and applied its template and the associated Microsoft Word *paragraph styles* for front and back matter, chapter openers, space breaks, place and date markers (such as *Berlin, 1942* at the beginning of a chapter or section), and *character styles* for italics, bold, small caps, and so on.[1] So even the unedited manuscript will be pretty clean (with some variation, of course) and "ready to go." If your client is an indie

---

1. Some publishers are still using inline codes, similar to HTML codes (such as <CN> for a chapter number and <BL> for a bulleted list) to mark up copy for the compositor, but this is becoming less and less common.

The Navigation Pane and the Style Area Pane

In Microsoft Word, two features are especially useful: the Navigation pane and the style area pane (see figure 2.1).[1] The screenshots shown here are in Microsoft Word 2019 for Windows. Figure 2.1a is a larger full-screen view showing the panes next to the text; figure 2.1b is an enlarged partial view.

The Navigation Pane

The Navigation pane (at far left in the figure) shows the outline levels that have been assigned to heading styles for chapter numbers and titles; in fiction this is most useful for showing you what chapter you're in and for quickly going to a different chapter by clicking its number or title in the Navigation pane. It also provides a quick way to skim chapter numbers and ensure that they are numbered and styled correctly. In Word 2019, the Navigation pane can be accessed on the View tab; you may find it convenient to learn the keyboard shortcut for your version to toggle it on and off.

The Style Area Pane

The style area pane (to the right of the Navigation pane in the figure), visible only in Draft or Outline view, shows you the paragraph style for each paragraph; this makes it easy to see, for example, if your chapter numbers, body text, and other elements are styled correctly. It's a little more difficult to access in Word 2019, with lots of clicking required: File > Options > Advanced > Display > Style area pane width in Draft and Outline views > [set desired width; 1 inch is usually sufficient]. (For ease of access, you can record two macros: one to set the

---

1. Note that the manuscript itself is in 16-point Verdana, the screen-optimized font I prefer to use while editing. The final version of the manuscript will be converted to fit the submission requirements of the agent or publisher, typically 12-point Times New Roman.

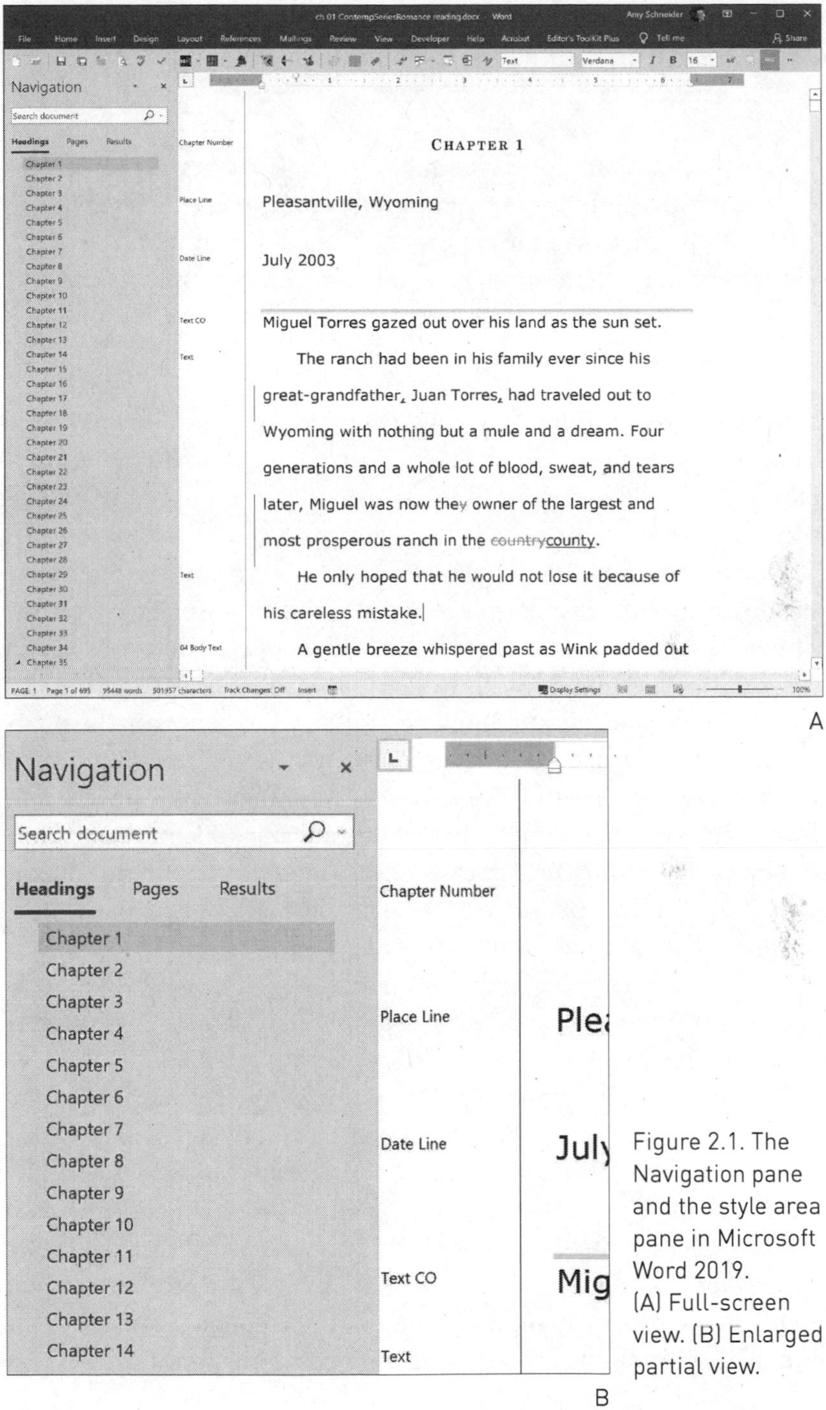

Figure 2.1. The Navigation pane and the style area pane in Microsoft Word 2019. (A) Full-screen view. (B) Enlarged partial view.

width at 1 inch to turn it on, and another setting the width at 0 inches to turn it off. Assign each to a keyboard shortcut to quickly enable and disable the style area pane.) Once the style area pane is open, you can drag the vertical rule right or left to change the width. (Note that the style area pane, which only shows you the currently applied styles, is different from the Styles dialog, where you can create, modify, and apply styles.)

author, the manuscript may have been through developmental or substantive editing (and a wise freelance copyeditor recommends or requires them before copyediting, so as not to end up trying to copy-edit what is really a first draft).

One of your first tasks when you receive a manuscript file (after saving the original in a safe place and saving a new working copy; see Appendix B: File Management) is to simply open it to confirm that it's complete and readable. If the chapters are numbered, check to see that the numbering is complete and in order, and that the number format is consistent. (Is it *21*, *Chapter 21*, *CHAPTER 21*, *Chapter Twenty-One*, or *Chapter Twenty-one*?) Scroll through quickly and check the text for weirdness that could indicate a file problem, such as obviously missing or truncated text. Contact the client immediately if the file does not seem to be in usable condition.

All manuscripts must include page numbers. However, in the age of on-screen editing, page numbering can change when a file is opened on different computers, in different programs, with different templates attached, or when extensive edits are made. So because fiction manuscripts are commonly a single file, it's more accurate and useful to use chapter numbers (if provided) to identify where the relevant text for notes on your style sheet is located in the manuscript and to help narrow searches for information if necessary. (See the sample style sheets in part II for examples.) If the chapters are not numbered—for example, if they have only descriptive titles—you may need to devise a temporary numbering scheme (with your client's permission), such as inserting temporary chapter numbers and instructing the client to delete them when the manuscript is ready for production. See the sidebar titled "The Navigation Pane and the Style Area Pane" for a discussion of two useful navigation and formatting tools in your Word workspace.

Specialized Editing Plug-Ins for Word

Spell check is one example of a basic, built-in tool that automates one of the mechanical aspects of copyediting. You can "power up" Word even more by using third-party tools designed especially for editors, such as Intelligent Editing's PerfectIt (intelligentediting.com) and the Editorium's Editor's ToolKit Plus (editorium.com).

PerfectIt is a customizable consistency checker that you can run on a document to check elements such as capitalization, hyphenation, spelling, and even house style. You can set up PerfectIt to define the style it will follow when checking your document (including *CMOS* style), and PerfectIt makes no changes unless you tell it to do so. Many editors run PerfectIt both before and after an edit. You can install PerfectIt directly in Microsoft Word for Windows or Mac.

Editor's ToolKit Plus (ETKPlus) is a suite of tools that install as a set of global templates in Microsoft Word for Windows or Mac. The tools that are most useful for fiction copyediting are Editor's ToolKit and FileCleaner. Editor's ToolKit provides shortcuts for functions such as managing Track Changes, navigating the document, and manipulating text during an edit; FileCleaner automates typographic cleanup of text before you begin copyediting.

You can learn more about these and other editing-specific tools for Word by joining editors' discussion groups via email and social media, both general groups and those for specific tools. The technology changes constantly, and the wise editor keeps up with these changes.

You might also do some cleanup procedures at this stage, especially if a publisher has not already done so. These can include running consistency-checking software and doing typographic cleanup such as replacing two spaces with one; removing extraneous tabs; standardizing font, margins, line spacing, indents, and so on; changing straight quotation marks to "smart" (curly) ones; and applying styles. One of the advantages of copyediting in Word is that you can use it to perform much of this mechanical "grunt work," so you can focus your time and energy on the parts of copyediting that require human judgment. Rather than using Word "out of the box," you can customize the Word interface using its built-in options, learn to create and use tools such as macros and templates to streamline your work, or install any of the plug-ins available to supplement Word's basic functions. If you're not familiar with macros for editors, see the Recommended Resources to get started. See also the sidebar titled "Specialized Editing Plug-Ins for Word" for a discussion of two useful plug-ins for copyeditors.

Setting up the style sheet

Your next consideration is the style sheet that you will create for this project. This section gives an overview of the style resources you may be using; see chapter 3 for details on how to decide on and record various points of general style.

Most publishers require copyeditors to create and provide a style sheet recording all of the style decisions for the manuscript. Indie authors may not be familiar with the concept of a style sheet; if your author is not, you can explain the purpose of the style sheet and how it can be useful to them as a reference document as they review your edits and in later production stages.

PUBLISHER HOUSE STYLE AND DICTIONARY

Publishers in the United States generally follow *The Chicago Manual of Style* (*CMOS*) and *Merriam-Webster's Collegiate Dictionary*, currently in its eleventh edition (*MW11*), for general style decisions. *Merriam-Webster Unabridged* and the *American Heritage Dictionary* (*AHD*) serve as secondary resources. All are available online. (See

Style Guides and Dictionaries for Australian, British, and Canadian English

The following references are commonly used resources for their respective varieties of English. See the Recommended Resources for publication details.

Australian English
Style guide: *The Australian Editing Handbook*, 3rd ed. (2014)
Dictionaries: *Australian Oxford Dictionary*, 2nd ed. (2005); *Oxford English Dictionary* (online)

British English
Style guide: *New Oxford Style Manual* (contains *New Hart's Rules* and the *New Oxford Dictionary for Writers and Editors*) (2016)
Dictionaries: *Oxford English Dictionary* (online); *Collins English Dictionary*, 13th ed. (2017; also online)

Canadian English
Style guides: *The Canadian Press Stylebook*, 18th ed. (2018); *Editing Canadian English*, 3rd ed. (2015)
Dictionaries: *Canadian Oxford Dictionary*, 2nd ed. (2005); *Oxford English Dictionary* (online)

the sidebar titled "Style Guides and Dictionaries for Australian, British, and Canadian English" for additional resources.)

Many publishers also have a house style guide particular to their organization; if they don't supply one, ask for it. Here you will find house style preferences, either where *CMOS* offers alternatives or where house style differs from *CMOS*. Save a copy and review it before beginning any work for that client.

PREVIOUS STYLE SHEET, IF PROVIDED

If you are editing for a publisher, you may also receive a style sheet (or more than one) from previous books by the same author, either previous stand-alone books or previous books in the same series. Either way, a previous style sheet, compiled by you or by someone else, is a useful guide to the author's preferences or to style decisions made by previous copyeditors. If you worked on the previous book and receive your own style sheet back, pay attention to changes that have been made after you submitted it. You might receive a previous style sheet as a Word document (with additions and changes tracked or highlighted) or as a PDF (with handwritten changes) created from the original Word document. Having the Word document makes it easy to copy information to your own fresh style sheet; if you receive the style sheet as a PDF (one that was created from a Word document and not scanned from hard copy), ask your client if they can also send the original Word document for ease of copying.

When you review the previous style sheet, mentally note anything that you want to begin addressing during the first pass. (See the section titled "Passes and Rounds" later in this chapter for a discussion of the difference between passes and rounds of editing.) For example, does the style sheet call for the serial comma? Most do, but some authors prefer to omit it. I'm a fan of the serial comma, so when it's omitted by choice, I need to pay attention. (See chapter 3 for more discussion of general punctuation style.) The previous style sheet also alerts you to other deliberate or unusual style choices before you begin.

If you are working on a book that's part of a series, you may receive (or request!) a PDF of the previous book in the series. This is useful for looking up issues that aren't covered on the style sheet. It may also contain handy items such as maps of fictional worlds, backstory that isn't provided in the current manuscript, and examples of unusual formatting. (See also the section titled "Series Style Sheets" later in this chapter.)

Publishers may also supply information such as genre, setting, audience, and publication date; the level of copyediting the project manager believes it needs; unusual choices the author has deliberately made; how receptive the author is to queries (see the discussion later in this chapter); or other notes, such as "For this book we are keeping UK spellings but Americanizing punctuation" or "This author has a quirky, casual style that should be maintained." Review these notes before beginning your first pass. If you are copyediting for an indie author, discuss unusual choices with the author ahead of time and agree on the details; this discussion may need to wait until after you have made a light reading pass through the manuscript and discovered the choices you'd like to clarify.

YOUR STYLE SHEET

Your style sheet for this new project will be a compilation of information that the client has supplied—house style, previous style sheets, notes about the book's particular style or author preferences—and information and style decisions that you collect and develop as you copyedit. You may find it helpful to create a style sheet template for each client, both as a starting point for new projects that have no previous guides and as a way to quickly review the client's style before beginning the edit. (See Appendix A: Style Sheet Templates for more information about the technical aspects of these tools, and see part II for details about the contents of a fiction style sheet.)

Before you start copyediting, if you've received a previous style sheet or notes about author preferences, add those items to the new style sheet. Style choices from a previous book or author preferences generally override house style and replace what's on your boilerplate—but check with your client if you're unsure.

If the front or back matter of the manuscript includes backstory, character descriptions, maps, information about aspects of the story's fictional world (such as magic, clan groups, paranormal elements and creatures, and animal species), a chronology, or other descriptive information for readers, lucky you! Copy that information to your style sheet. You'll spend less time trying to figure out the details if the author has already laid it out for you. You can also ask the author (or have the project manager ask) if they have created such materials but not included them in the manuscript and are willing to share them for your reference.

See the pattern here? You're building a main reference guide for everything about this manuscript. All of the available information about the world, its characters, its places, its history and timeline, and its fictional elements goes on the style sheet, because it can't be looked up anywhere else. This prepopulated style sheet is your starting point; you'll fill in the rest as you copyedit.

SERIES STYLE SHEETS

Style sheets for novels that are part of a series present a challenge: the need to impose consistency not just within the current book but also with previous books in the series. Elements in previously published books cannot be revised; for example, if Arturo was six feet tall in book 1, he can't be five foot seven in book 3 (barring magical transformation!). We'll discuss more specific examples in part II. For now, let's look at how to organize style points and story facts across a series.

If you are lucky enough to be the copyeditor of the first book in a series as well as the ones that follow it, great! Simply create a new style sheet when you edit book 1. When you start working on book 2, open the style sheet from book 1 (which you archived when you finished book 1; see Appendix B: File Management), save a copy in the project folder for book 2, change the title and other information, and do the edit. Save the completed style sheet for book 2. When you start working on book 3, open the style sheet from book 2 . . . and so on.

What if you didn't work on the previous book? The process is similar. Start with your blank style sheet and add information from style sheets or other notes supplied from the previous book, then continue with the edit as usual. You'll still be able to maintain cross-book consistency by using the previous book's information that you added to the style sheet. If you receive a PDF of the previous book, search that to check particular style points as needed. If you don't have the PDF, Amazon's "Look Inside" feature can be useful if the book is sold there; Google Books is also an option, though often less useful for fiction. You can also see if your local library has an ebook version that you can check out for reference.

Keeping track of story facts that appeared in previous books is important; although you can tweak a fact in chapter 3 to make it consistent with a fact in chapter 26, you can't change something in book 2 (which is already published) to match up with book 3, which you're working on right now. So you'll need to figure out how to identify on your style sheet published facts that can't be changed. Some options are identifying them with a code (such as a few letters representing the previous book's title, with a note added to the style sheet); tagging information from the current book with a chapter number (if provided); or using font color or highlighting to distinguish established and new information. In the general style section, you can add "(series style)" or "(au pref)" after an entry to indicate that it should not be changed. I use all of these as needed; feel free to develop your own system. (See figures 3.1, 4.1, and 4.2 for examples.)

When possible, maintain style choices that have already been established; however, use your judgment if a previous decision appears to be a mistake and may need to be corrected or if the author appears to have changed their mind in the middle of a series. You may need to consult with the author or publisher and get a ruling on how to proceed.

If you find an inconsistency across books, your options depend on the nature of the problem. If you see a simple solution, make the change and insert a query explaining why it's needed and ask the author to approve it. For example, if Kala had a tattoo on her right shoulder in the previous book, but now it's on her left shoulder (and this fact does not affect the plot), that can be fixed with a simple one-word change and a query noting the reason.

However, sometimes the error would require rewriting a scene, involves a critical plot point, or is too entrenched in the current story and may have to be ignored this late in the editorial process. In such cases, you should still write a query bringing the issue to the author's attention. They may see a solution that you haven't thought of, or they may be okay with letting it slide. That's the author's choice to make.

When you have finished the edit, you may have some "leftover" characters or places on your style sheet that did not appear or were not mentioned in the current book. I recommend leaving these in their own lists at the end of their respective sections (Characters and Places) with a descriptive header (such as "Characters from [the] previous book[s]"), in case they show up in a future book (see figures 4.1

and 4.2). Similarly, keep any general terms or style choices that did not appear or apply in this book in the general style section, to help ensure consistency across future books.

ANTHOLOGIES

Anthologies present a slightly different situation. The publisher may want the editor to apply an overall house style (such as US spelling and punctuation) but allow each story to maintain its own internal style for each author (such as varying levels of formality in grammar and syntax). A practical solution is to cite the house style guide at the top of the style sheet and create separate mini-sections for each story, with variations from the overall general style and brief sections for characters, places, and timeline (see figure 2.2). When the edit is complete, format each story's section so it fits on its own page(s), so the style sheet can be easily divided and the sections distributed to each author for review. (Be flexible, though; as I write this, I am copy-editing an anthology of stories by a single author that are all set in the world of her long-running book series, with the same characters, invented elements, and style choices running across multiple stories. I'm treating it as a single book and breaking out only a separate time-line for each story.)

Even though you are dealing with a shorter story, you may be surprised by plot issues you can pick up by tracking the same things you track in a novel-length manuscript.

Diving into the edit

The manuscript is cleaned up and formatted, you've reviewed house style and author preferences, and it's time to start your first pass. But wait! First let's clarify the difference between passes and rounds.

PASSES AND ROUNDS

The definitions of passes and rounds of editing are frequently confused, particularly when negotiating with indie authors, where the number of rounds often figures into the cost estimate. So ensuring that everyone is working with the same definitions is important.

A *pass* is one "trip" through a manuscript to perform a particular task, and it can have varying levels of intensity. Most manuscripts

STYLE SHEET (5/6/2022)
Some Amazing Short Stories (anthology)
Project Manager: Janis Doe   Copyeditor: Amy J. Schneider

References

The Fruity Publishing Group House Style Guide
Chicago Manual of Style, 17th edition
Merriam-Webster's Collegiate Dictionary, 11th edition (online)

"Pomegranate Surprise" by Shea Walker

Characters

Courtney McLeod (Court) (she): sandy blond hair
Mom (Rachel) (she): history teacher at Ashland Academy
Dad (Alan) (he): architect
Ellen (she): Courtney's sister; dark hair

Kali (she): tall, thin; dark curly hair; brown eyes; only child
Shira (she): Kali's girlfriend; long auburn/blond (? queried in ms.) hair; works at the Beanery
Amma (she): Kali's grandmother; petite

Bonita (she)
Mrs. Rivas (she): Courtney's neighbor

Barbra Streisand (she)
Rivers Cuomo (he)
Adele (she)

Places

Kali's house: tiny front porch; 2 stories; painted white wood
        small back yard with patio
        sunny kitchen; gas stove, painted cabinets
        15-minute walk from the Beanery

the Beanery: coffeehouse
Starbucks: across town
Ashland Academy: on 9 acres; founded 50 years ago

Sample Anthology Style Sheet, page 1 of 6

Figure 2.2. Sample anthology style sheet

require at least two full passes in which the editor reads every word: a lighter "reading" pass and a heavier "detailed editing" pass. During other, quicker passes, the editor might pay attention only to certain things (see the section titled "Third Pass: Tidying Up" later in this chapter for examples). Consider the analogy of cleaning your house or apartment. First, you pick up your stray belongings and put them away. Then you do a "pass" to dust, and another to sweep, vacuum, and mop. A pass to clean the windows if you're feeling ambitious.

Timeline

- story begins
- late that afternoon; Ellen goes to work
- tomorrow is Saturday

- next morning
- late morning
- Shira is working all weekend
- 7:30 pm
- Ellen due home around 9 pm
- 11 am

- next day; Shira is home **(? queried in ms.)**

Numbers

seven thirty (time)

Abbreviations

DIY   do it yourself
FDR   Franklin Delano Roosevelt

Punctuation

serial comma
a you've-got-to-be-kidding-me look
jet-black (a)

oh no, oh yeah

Typography

labels small caps
in address: sis, babe, sweetie

Word List

back seat
barbecue (n)
Burger Bob's (tm)
email (a, n, v)
geez (interj)
Girl Scout (n)
goodbye (n)
gray (a)
hang on to (v)
hangry (a)
Internet (n)
jet pack (n)
livestream (v)
man bun (n)
Mocha Madness (drink)
okay (adv)
till (prep)
trade-off (n)
tsked (v)
Wi-Fi (n)
yellow pages (n)
zeros (pl n)

Sample Anthology Style Sheet, page 2 of 6

Maybe you replace the dead lightbulbs and refill the soap dispensers. And finally, you arrange the knickknacks just so and finish the job with a spritz of air freshener. Done! That's six passes.

A *round* of editing begins when the editor receives the manuscript and ends when the editor returns it to the client for review. A round usually consists of multiple passes, as described in the preceding paragraph. For fiction copyediting, most publishers require only one round: the copyeditor receives the manuscript, edits it (in multiple

---

"Cherry Jubilee" by Phoebe Hunter

Characters

Alanah Sinclair (she): long dark curls halfway down her back; wide-set eyes; Black
Alanah's mom (she): owns a florist shop
"Samson"/"Sammy": beagle; male; age 2

Roberta (she): Alanah's best friend

Tyson (they): buzzed black hair; tat sleeves on both arms; started playing guitar at age 7; lessons
    on Fridays
Dad (he): travels a lot for business

Donald (he): Tyson's guitar teacher
Selma (she): another guitar student; blue eyes; wears heavy makeup

Places

Northern California

Alanah's house: on Caldwell Avenue; large fenced yard; her bedroom is upstairs

Donald's studio: in a strip mall; row of practice rooms on the left side; used instruments for sale
    on right side; old-fashioned cash register

Timeline

• Wednesday morning; Alanah meets Tyson

• 2 days later (Friday)
• Tyson goes to their weekly lesson
• almost sunset

• 10 am next day (Saturday); rainy
• Sammy gets loose

• next morning (Sunday); Sammy shows up

Numbers

ten a.m. (time)
24/7

Sample Anthology Style Sheet, page 3 of 6

---

passes) and inserts queries (discussed later in this chapter), returns it to the publisher, and never sees it again. Some publishers also hire the same copyeditor for a cleanup round (see "Cleanup/review" later in this chapter). When a copyeditor is working with an indie author, these two rounds of editing are recommended, plus more if the author and copyeditor agree that more are needed. Continuing with our cleaning analogy, every time you clean your house is a round of cleaning, with separate passes for each task.

Abbreviations

ASAP as soon as possible
vs.   versus

Punctuation

serial comma   ,
bloodred (a)
oh shit; oh god

Typography

direct thought, imagined dialogue italic
words as words italic
letters as shapes roman, cap:
            her mouth formed an O
text messages italic

in address: buddy, kiddo, sir

Mr. No-Show (epithet)
I wanted to say yes

spell it A-L-A-N-A-H

Usage

OK to ignore *who/whom* distinction

Miscellaneous

"Listen to the Silence" (song)
Black

Word List

backward (adv)
dive-bomb (v)
dominoes (pl n)
fettuccine (n)
floofy (a)
goodbye (n)
gray (a, n)
hawk a loogie (a)
key card (n)
loop-the-loop (v)
off-course (pa)
okay (adv)
Selma-speak (n)
showier (a)
sicced (v)
takeout (n)
toward (prep)
T-shirt (n)
video call (n)

Sample Anthology Style Sheet, page 4 of 6

Therefore, a round of editing consists of multiple passes. The editor charges more for more rounds, but the number of passes is included in each round and varies depending on whatever issues the editor encounters during the edit.

WHICH PASS FIRST?

You can approach the manuscript in a couple of ways. One method is to do the "light pass" first (just reading the story, doing light copy-

---

"Nectarine Delight" by Jareth Rudd

Characters

Wiley (he/they): queer; came out 5 years ago; sophomore at Rigby College
Ellis (they): Wiley's romantic partner; tall and thin

Mr. Simmons (he): Wiley's landlord
Kasey (she) and Donnell (he): live across the hall from Wiley
Mia Fernandez (she): lives down the hall; senior

Leela Arnold (she): petite; spiky blue/teal (? queried in ms.) hair; round face; shorter than
      Wiley; works at the organic food co-op
"Ripley": black lab; male
Cole Baxter (he): Leela's uncle; owns the co-op

gray-haired woman pushing a walker (she)
man wearing a Wolverines jersey (he)

Anabella/Anabelle (she) (? queried in ms.)

Beyoncé (she)

Places

Stewart Avenue: "the strip"; 6 blocks south of the co-op
14th Street: runs north and south
Langley (street): intersects with Stewart Avenue

the co-op: run-down brick building

"the Runaround": big traffic circle near the college

Sample Anthology Style Sheet, page 5 of 6

editing that requires no style decisions) and the "main pass" second (doing the word-for-word edit, compiling the style sheet, writing queries); another method is main pass first, light pass second. I prefer to do the lighter pass first, then the detailed edit, and this is the method that I recommend. Why? An initial light reading pass enables the copyeditor to become familiar with the story and the characters, the author's voice, and issues to watch for (such as names that are spelled inconsistently, repeated pet phrases, and possible plot issues). At the

---

Timeline

• morning
• that night; 8:30 pm

• about 4 days later

• next morning; hot and sunny

• a week later; 4 am
• 9 am
• late afternoon

Numbers

three p.m.; five-something (time)
between 14th and 15th streets
a full one-eighty
twenty-four-seven

Punctuation

serial comma

Typography

direct thought, imagined dialogue italic
words as words italic
letters as letters italic
text messages italic

in address: buddy
my uncle Cole

the send button

oh my god; I hope to god
oh no you didn't

say please

Usage

because traffic

Miscellaneous

Urban Assault (game/app)

Word List

Fraser fir (n)
bingeing (v)
Chihuahua (n)
conversate (v)
gray (a, n)
health care (a, n)
goldendoodle (n)
whatcha (what are you)
mini-fridge (n)
mustache (n)
Sun Belt, the (n)
other team, the (n)
shape-shift (v)

Sample Anthology Style Sheet, page 6 of 6

---

same time, the copyeditor learns about potential *red herrings* (false clues deliberately planted to mislead the reader), people who are not what they seem, and so on, so that they can watch for related plot holes during the second pass and fix them accordingly. Doing the detailed edit first without foreknowledge of the story and general style creates the potential for too much rework and possible missed errors during a second lighter pass.

You can also break up these passes into chunks that make sense for you. Before you begin your preliminary reading pass, you might review your preliminary style sheet and run search-and-replace for things like *toward/towards*, serial commas, and other no-decision style issues so they don't distract you when you're reading for things like voice and plot. You might do a separate pass for timeline issues, especially if the timeline is complex or has obvious problems. You might make a pass to review a particular character's quirky dialogue for consistency. As you gain experience, you may add tasks to your checklist—or realize that a task is more time-consuming than it's worth or can be combined with a different task.

If you are new to fiction copyediting, experiment to find out which method works best for you. Since I work from a light edit to a detailed edit, that is the process I describe in this chapter.

FIRST PASS: GET THE BONBONS . . .
The initial light reading pass is my favorite part of copyediting a novel. Laptop: check. Couch, pillow, and blankie: check. Snacks: check. A doggo or two at my feet: check. This is the image that many people have of what copyediting fiction entails, and although it's not the whole picture, it's an important (and fun!) part. You might print out the manuscript and write notes in the margins, or read it on your tablet. Whatever works for you!

Step one: Just read it! Open the manuscript file (or get comfy with your printout) and read it mostly just as you would read for pleasure. Get to know the characters, the setting, the plot, the author's writing style. During this pass, make no style decisions. (You can have the style sheet handy if you like, but only for quick reference.) As Karen Judd writes, this pass is primarily for discovering how the story turns out. You may wear your metaphorical copyediting hat, but don't get bogged down in making and recording style decisions while you are acquainting yourself with the story and general style.

You'll probably notice things that you want to check in more depth later: *Wasn't this character's name different before? Note to self: pay attention to Malia/Maliya on second pass. (Flag* it with a highlighted note to yourself in the manuscript, if that helps you remember.) Some questions may be answered later as you read on. At this point I don't correct anything that might need a query—even an "AU: OK?"—

because I don't want to derail myself. If anything, I simply flag it and move on.

Start cleaning things up so you can concentrate on the big stuff during the second pass. Fix things that are outright, indisputable errors: wrong word choice (such as *hoard* for *horde*), punctuation errors (such as double periods), and so on. At this stage, you can also correct obvious typographic glitches, such as deleting extraneous spaces, moving commas and periods inside quotation marks (for US punctuation style), and converting multiple hyphens to en or em dashes. (Note: Some publishers require that all such changes be tracked; others allow untracked routine changes like these that do not require author approval, but they may ask the copyeditor to supply a list of the types of changes that were made silently. Check with your project manager before proceeding.)

You probably won't catch all of these minor glitches on the first pass, and that's okay. It's not meant to be a comprehensive pass. This is one case where you're actually doing what many laypeople think copyeditors do: reading the latest thriller or steamy romance and fixing typos. We know that the heavy lifting comes later.

You can make simple style fixes per previous or house style: applying (or removing) the serial comma, styling words used as words (either italic, or roman in quotation marks), applying UK or US spelling, and so on. But this is not the time for edits that require research or a major decision, especially anything that would go on the style sheet, because you are still getting a feel for the overall work; you may find that a choice you made early in the book is overridden later on, causing extra work to go back and revert changes that may not be easily or quickly found.

You may notice issues you'll want to deal with on the next pass: possible inconsistencies, repetitive pet phrases, types of errors that occur frequently, and so on. Second-Pass Copyeditor (you) will thank First-Pass Copyeditor (also you) for making mental notes or even a quick highlighted note in the manuscript, to be removed later when the issue is resolved.

This is also a good time to mentally note the level of detail in the manuscript. Are there lots of proper names (people, places, objects, trademarks)? Detailed descriptions of people, places, objects, timeline, and plot? Extensive background or historical information? Knowing how much detail is involved helps you estimate how long the second pass will take and determine how much detail you'll record on your style sheet; the more detail, the more potential for inconsistencies to slip through.

SECOND PASS: THE BIG EDIT

We've reached the main event: the detailed copyediting pass. This is where you read the manuscript word by word, make all your style decisions and editorial revisions, and compile the style sheet. You'll have the manuscript open in one window and your style sheet open in another, frequently going back and forth between them. (See Appendix C: Multiple Monitors for advice on an efficient way to work in multiple documents at once.)

During the first pass, you may have flagged items to review and resolve during the second pass. Similarly, you may flag other issues that reveal themselves during the second pass, to review and resolve after completing the second pass (or, if you cannot resolve them, to ask the author to do so).

What goes into a fiction style sheet? A fiction style sheet contains much of what goes into a nonfiction style sheet but also several elements that are unique to fiction. In addition to notes about editorial style choices, most publishers expect (at minimum) a list of character names, a list of places mentioned in the story, and a chronology or timeline. Here's a brief overview of the sections of a fiction style sheet, which are covered in more detail in part II.

- *General style* (chapter 3): Just as for nonfiction, you'll track treatment of numbers (for example, they are usually spelled out in dialogue, but not always). You'll keep a list of abbreviations for both real and fictional entities. How is dialogue punctuated? How are internal thoughts, telepathic dialogue, remembered speech, handwriting, text messages, and so on being treated? These decisions go in the general style section. Which terms of address are capped (*Officer, Detective*) and which are not (*ma'am, sweetheart*)? These are only a few of the style decisions covered in chapter 3. The

author may choose one style or another for each point. Or
the publisher may request that the author's style be changed.
Because these choices are so fluid in fiction, you need to record
them for each book.

- *Characters* (chapter 4): A list of characters is a good start, but
you can catch a lot of problems by going a bit further. Some
authors keep rigorous track of their characters' attributes—
but many do not. Or they make changes but don't catch every
instance. Marcel becomes Malcolm. Julie's eyes change color
from blue to green. Tariq is left-handed but wears a golf glove
on his left hand (oops—most golfers wear the glove on their
nondominant hand; query time!). Lee is single and an only
child—so how is it that they have a niece? Back when you
edited book 1 in the series, you noted that Claude could read
ancient Sumerian, but now in book 3 he has mysteriously lost
that ability. Time to query! See chapter 4 for a comprehensive
discussion of character traits to track.

- *Places* (chapter 5): As with characters, a simple list provides
a basic reference, but tracking the details of both real and
fictional locations often reveals glitches that you might not
spot otherwise. Nell's bedroom is on the second floor, and
the walls are painted blue. Sticksville is twenty-five miles
from Cityscape. The tree on the west side of the park is a
magnificent oak. And so on. So when Nell walks in the front
door of her cottage and down the hall to her green bedroom,
that's an oops that needs attention. Chapter 5 covers the ins
and outs (ha!) of tracking details about places.

- *Timeline and plot* (chapter 6): The level of detail here varies.
Some authors use only vague time markers (*a few days later*; *by
spring*), if any. Others are more specific, mentioning dates, days
of the week, and times of day. Record all references to time,
whether vague or specific: Carlos's birthday is next month.
The Friday-night knitting club meets tomorrow (in which case
today had better be Thursday). The last mention of time today
was nine a.m.; has the action moved along sufficiently that it
can now be midnight? Chapter 6 describes different methods
you can use to format a timeline and how to spot problems.

How do I decide what information to put where? Sometimes it's obvious where information gleaned from the manuscript should go on the style sheet, and other times not so much. For example:

> The slender teenage girl ran a hand through her short blond hair, her crystal-blue eyes brimming with tears. Her nametag read *Alison*.

This is all clearly character information, and it should go under an entry for Alison under "Characters": teenage girl; short blond hair, blue eyes; slender (see chapter 4).

But what about this:

> Doug's fourth-floor apartment had served his needs perfectly well in the six years since he'd moved to the Bronx.

Should Doug's apartment be part of his character description, or should it be an entry under "Places"? What about the fact that he moved into it six years ago? Is that also a character description, or should it go on the timeline?

This is where your first pass guides you. After your first pass through the manuscript, you'll know (for example) that there is no other description of Doug's apartment and that the entire story takes place in the Bronx over a couple of months. This tells you that this information probably won't need close tracking under "Places" or on the timeline, so a one-line entry under Doug under "Characters" should suffice:

moved into his 4th-floor apartment in the Bronx 6 years ago

Conversely, the first pass might have revealed that the middle part of the story revolves around Doug and his neighbors, who all live in apartments on different floors in the same building, described in rich detail along with other buildings in the neighborhood; that the story spans Doug's life from his childhood through middle age; and that he lived in four different cities during that time. In that case, it makes better sense to create several entries: (1) a main entry under "Places" for the Bronx, with a subentry for Doug's apartment building that contains a description of his apartment specifically (and will be expanded during the edit to include the other apartments); (2) an entry on the timeline showing that Doug moved to the Bronx six years ago; and (3) depending on other information given, an entry under "Characters" showing that Doug moved to the Bronx six years ago, and if his age at the time is known or can be inferred, including that as well. (We'll go into this process in more detail in part II.)

At the same time, don't sweat too much about where you put things. As long as it seems logical, the important part is to get it down on the style sheet. Be flexible; you may change your mind as new information presents itself and decide to move things around.

Does it matter whether information comes from dialogue or narration? Story details can be revealed in both. Dialogue is a rich source of information as the characters observe their world and talk to each other. However, when pulling information from dialogue, consider the source. Is the character lying or confused? Are things not as they seem at first, because the truth is revealed later? You may need to annotate certain facts as you go: Dr. Blaine: (says she) graduated from medical school in 1976 (but she actually flunked out). Facts can also change throughout the story: hair grows and is cut or dyed, castles crumble from neglect, personal relationships and situations change. Be flexible; you may need to adjust your notes as the story progresses.

Other second-pass concerns. In addition to characters, places, and timeline/plot, fiction has other aspects that distinguish it from most nonfiction; these are covered in more detail in part III. Chapter 1 discussed the relaxation of formal language rules; grammar, usage, and other language issues specific to fiction are discussed in chapter 7. Dialogue is allowed even more leeway than narration, but first-person narration (a form of dialogue) can be informal as well. Diction, accents, and grammar, as well as appropriate use of punctuation and dialogue tags, all convey each character's voice via dialogue, the topic of chapter 8. Finally, ensuring that the fictional world of the story is consistent with the real world (as appropriate) is covered in chapter 9.

THIRD PASS: TIDYING UP

After you complete the main edit, you'll probably have multiple little notes to yourself remaining in the manuscript, or a separate list of things you want to go back and check. Publishers generally do not pay rates that allow for a third complete reading pass; instead, you might do multiple mini-passes:

- Search for things you've flagged to check later: names that are spelled inconsistently, facts that need to be researched, and items that require feedback from the client are a few examples.
- Review all of your queries for typos, accuracy, and tact, and ensure that you haven't left in any queries about issues that were resolved later. (See the section on queries later in this chapter to learn about writing thoughtful and helpful queries.)
- Check chapter heads, place and date lines (*San Francisco / Thursday, 9:30 a.m.*), letters, and other repeated elements for consistency. (It often helps to copy recurring elements like place and date lines to your style sheet, so you can compare them as you edit, choose a style, and create generic examples for the style sheet when the edit is complete.)
- Do a final search for various little elements you might have forgotten. For example, among other things, I always search for &&&, the string I use to mark my stopping point whenever I take a work break, leave my current position in the manuscript to check something elsewhere, or stop work for the day; the Word character style I use for flags to myself (some copyeditors use highlighting for this); double spaces and periods; and spaces around paragraph marks.

When you've cleared all notes to yourself and finalized the queries, it's time to run your final cleanup routines.

- *Spell check:* If you do nothing else at this point, run a spell check! Most publishers require it as a final step, and for good reason. Typos, missing spaces, and other glitches slip past even the sharpest copyeditor.
- *Consistency check:* Consistency-checking software such as PerfectIt (see the Recommended Resources) is excellent for picking up inconsistencies in hyphenation, capitalization, numbers, style, and many other areas. As with spell check, you'll be surprised by how much it picks up, and grateful that

it has your back. There can be a bit of a learning curve, but it's well worth the investment.

After you've gotten the manuscript into its final form, save it as a new file, using the naming convention your client has specified, if any. If your client doesn't require a particular naming style, give the file a name that clearly identifies the contents and the editing stage (see Appendix B: File Management for examples).

Always clean up your style sheet as well. Read it closely for typos and run spell check; check the organization; and finalize the formatting to make it look sharp for your client. Your style sheet will be passed along to other people in the production process (such as the author, publisher, production editor, proofreader, and compositor, and those who work on future books in a series); it represents you and your work, and you'll want to put your best foot forward.

Finally, write any notes you have for the client. For a publisher, this may be a brief email with general summarizing comments—for example, "Thanks for sending this project my way. The story really had me on the edge of my seat! Please note that I found several timeline issues that need attention. The copyedited manuscript and my style sheet and invoice are attached." This is also the place to query sensitive issues that you don't want to address directly with the author in the manuscript but want to bring to the publisher's attention. (See chapter 1 and the section on queries later in this chapter, as well as the section titled "Conscious language" in chapter 7.)

If your client is an indie author, your editorial letter may go into more detail: explaining your approach to edits and queries, explaining the style sheet and its purpose, and anything that you feel, based on your previous conversations and relationship with the author, will help them understand the copyediting process.

Whew! Now you can send the manuscript, style sheet, and cover note to your client, along with your invoice, and put your feet up and relax. At least until it's time to start the next project.

CLEANUP/REVIEW

But wait! Sometimes you'll be doing the final cleanup as well. After the author has reviewed the edited manuscript, answered the queries, and perhaps made a few more minor revisions, and any other outstanding issues have been resolved, someone needs to go through the manuscript and incorporate all those changes to produce a clean manuscript for the next production stage. Sometimes someone at the publisher does this task, such as the project manager. And sometimes they send it back to the copyeditor—you!

This final round is not a full word-by-word read but only a look at the changes. Review all tracked edits and the author's responses to ensure that revisions have been made correctly, do not introduce errors (such as typos, missing spaces, or syntax errors such as subject/verb mismatch), and conform to the style sheet. Accept each tracked change if the revision is correct; reject it if the author has requested that it be stetted or if the change introduces an error. Read newly inserted text as closely as you read the manuscript the first time, ensuring that it is mechanically and stylistically correct and flows smoothly with its surrounding text. When you have resolved each comment, delete it. When your substantive review is complete, do a few checks to tidy up (just as you did after your third pass): run a final spell check for typos and search for double spaces, double periods, spaces before and after paragraph marks, comment delimiters such as brackets, and so on. Your final product will be a clean file with no tracked changes and no comments or inline queries, ready for the compositor.

Doing cleanup can be a little scary because you can see how the author reacted to your edits. But it can also be educational and make you a better copyeditor. You'll see where you could have explained an edit better so the author could understand why you made it, instead of rejecting it out of hand. You'll see where you could have been a little more tactful, or where your careful consideration of your wording hit just the right tone on a sensitive query. You'll see where the author was right to stet your edit, and you'll consider that style issue more carefully next time. And hopefully, you'll mostly have the joy of knowing that the author was grateful for your careful and thorough attention to their manuscript and that you're on the right path.

A word about backup

We've seen the scary stories, and perhaps lived them: an accidental deletion, a corrupted file, damaged or stolen hardware. It's not a matter of *if* your hard drive will die, but *when*. The horror! But a solid backup routine changes "Oh, $#@&!" to "Ho-hum."

Saving progressive versions of files (which I hope you are already doing; see Appendix B: File Management) is only the beginning; you should also keep backup copies of your files in separate locations. Backup experts say that *a backup that's next to your computer is not a backup*. That external hard drive sitting next to your computer can be damaged in a fire or storm or stolen in a burglary along with your computer. Set up a reliable, robust backup system and stick to it, whether you use cloud-based backup, physical backup (multiple external drives rotated between your office and a separate location; I use my safe-deposit box and swap drives every few weeks), or a combination. (Relying on background tools alone, such as autosave or Word's Version History, is a recipe for disaster.) Backup storage is cheap; it's easy to set up regular automated backups of your entire system (don't try to remember where every file you might need is stored; just grab everything!). When you're done working for the day, save your active files to the cloud or a USB drive (or both); if your computer is toast the next morning, you can simply pull your backups and keep working. (You'll pull them to your backup computer. Backup hardware is just as important as backup files. Ask me how I know.) It's nearly impossible to have too many backups.

Queries

Let's talk about how to write *queries*. The most important part of your fiction copyeditor's uniform is your kid gloves. Remember that author you got to know earlier? They are a person who has sent their creation out into the world; the words on your screen are the author's pride and joy, and they may be feeling vulnerable when they receive the marked-up manuscript. You'll need to show the author that you're working *with* them to make their book the best it can be.

As you copyedit, you may need to flag problems by inserting *comment queries* (using a commenting function) or *inline queries* (inserting your query directly in the text), highlighting repetitive issues in the manuscript, or writing a separate note to the author or project manager. Query carefully, respectfully, and tactfully; here are some guidelines.

- First and foremost, focus on the needs of the story and the reader. Explain why readers might be confused or perceive something as a mistake.

  AU: Readers may be confused by this, because _____.
  [suggest alternative wording or other solution]
  AU: But in Ch. 10, Jeremy is the one who got sick—? (The wording here makes it sound like someone else got sick.)

- Be gentle; ask, don't tell. Phrase queries as questions and suggestions, not imperatives.

  AU: This seems to be the first mention of bipolar disorder; perhaps it should be brought in earlier?

- After asking your question, explain the reason for your query in parentheses to soften the tone.

  AU: OK as edited? (A class-action suit is filed on behalf of a large group of people, such as users of a certain product, not one person.)

- When the solution isn't obvious or requires author input, suggest revisions if you can and explain the reason, rather than making the change outright. ("It's not your book.") Authors are often more receptive to revision if you give them options instead of making them figure out what to do.

  AU: "Prone" generally indicates lying on the stomach; perhaps substitute "reclining" or similar?

- Use words like *perhaps* and *consider* to make it clear that you are suggesting, not commanding.

  AU: This phrasing seems a bit odd; perhaps the arm should be identified as a left arm on first mention, and change to just "index finger" here?

> AU: Consider having just a single exclamation point here, and perhaps add italics instead?

- Ask whether an unusual word choice was intentional; explain why it might look wrong to readers, or why you suspect it might be a typo for something else, and suggest alternatives.

> AU: Is "yucky" intentional here? (The term seems overly casual compared to Camilla's usually formal choice of vocabulary in narration from her point of view. Would something like "foul" or "repellent" work better?)
>
> AU: Did you perhaps mean "walking"? (Either "waking" or "walking" works here; just checking in case this was a typo.)
>
> AU: My first thought on reading this name was, "Oh, like the blues singer." OK to keep this coincidental name, or might readers be distracted by it? (Since it's a minor character, a name change would be simple to do.)

- Instead of saying that something is wrong in chapter 23 because it was different in chapter 5, ask whether the discrepancy is a contradiction if the difference is ambiguous.

> AU: Dorothy's hair is described as blond here in chapter 23, but she was a redhead in chapter 5; is this a contradiction? (Is she a strawberry blonde, or has she colored her hair?) Please clarify.

- Alternatively, if both conditions cannot be true and it's not clear which one the author intended, ask which one is correct. (Maybe the author changed their mind halfway through, and chapter 8 is wrong and chapter 31 is right.)

> AU: In chapter 8 he was born and raised in Morocco, but here in chapter 31 he says he was born in Spain; which is correct?

- Tread with special caution when copyediting dialogue (see also chapter 8):

AU: Della's speech pattern changed here; was this
    intentional? Or is my edit for consistency OK?

- When you encounter repeated issues throughout a
manuscript—a name spelled multiple ways, pet phrases
(see chapter 7), uncertainty about whether a term should
be capped or italicized everywhere—it's less intrusive and
overwhelming to insert a *global query* at the first instance,
explaining the issue and letting the author know what action
you suggest, rather than adding a separate query at every
instance. If the issue isn't easily searchable (for example, if the
problem wording varies), include a note telling the author that
you have highlighted each instance throughout.

GLOBAL QUERY: Should "the Prime" be capitalized
    throughout?
GLOBAL QUERY: There are various references throughout to
    how long Dev was imprisoned, ranging from 15 to 22 years,
    and it's not clear which figure is correct. I've highlighted
    them throughout; please review and make them consistent.

- Keep queries professional, but sometimes you can have a little
fun, in the interest of making a friendly connection with the
author.

AU: Is the preceding proliferation of P-words premeditated?
    Or would you prefer to reduce the alliteration?

- It's also fine to insert a compliment or a pleasant personal
note, especially if you don't have direct contact with the
author or if it's a heavy edit, to connect with the author
a little, provide a little positive feedback, and lighten the
often daunting task of reviewing your edits. However,
make sure that your tone comes across as professional and
respectful.

AU: My hometown! Your description is perfect.
AU: I laughed out loud at this! Cameron is such a great
    character.

- Use plain language when describing or explaining grammar and usage issues. Keep technical explanations to a minimum; if you must use one, keep it simple. Pull out the grammar terms only when necessary to make your point.

  AU: Revised to fix the dangling modifier; OK? (Sir Trevor was not stamping his hoof; his horse was.)

- During your final pass, review your queries for typos, clarity, and tone, and check whether any of them were resolved at a later point during the edit.

When you are working with a publisher and do not have direct author contact, you may have a query of a sensitive nature that would be uncomfortable to bring up with the author directly, or a question that needs to be addressed before you proceed with the edit. Here are some examples:

- The style sheet from a previous book in the series gives instructions that contradict what has been done in the current manuscript, and you would like clarification on how to treat that element because fixing it after the edit would be time-consuming.
- You feel that a character or situation may be perceived as offensive or inflammatory. (See the section titled "Conscious language" in chapter 7.)
- You've spotted a major plot hole that would involve extensive rewriting.

In such cases, it's best to discuss the issue with your project manager and ask them how they would like to proceed. They may agree with your assessment and ask you to hold off on editing until they resolve the issue. They may agree but ask you to complete the edit and flag problem areas either directly in the manuscript or in a cover note, so they can resolve the issue later. They may agree but say that there's nothing they can do about it at this point. Or they may say that they don't feel it's a problem, or it's already been discussed and they have decided to leave it as is.

Proofreading fiction

Proofreading fiction for publishers generally consists of checking typeset pages against the edited manuscript to ensure that all corrections were properly made, that no outright errors remain or have been introduced, and that the layout conforms to the design and to good typographic style and conventions. (See *CMOS* for a deeper description. If you are proofreading for an indie author, the process may be different, depending on your agreement with the client.) Proofreading of typeset pages can be done on paper or (more commonly) directly on a PDF in a program such as Adobe Acrobat. There may be several iterations of proofs, such as a first pass immediately after copyediting and author review and then a second pass after first proofs are corrected to catch any remaining issues. A proof pass may be in-depth, consisting of checking each correction in the manuscript against the proof; it may be simply slugging (quickly checking that all heads, paragraphs, and other elements are present) and then doing a cold read (just reading the text without referring to the manuscript unless clarification is needed); or the proofreader may be asked to simply do a cold read and may not even receive the manuscript. The proofreader may also receive the copyeditor's style sheet and/or the PDF of the previous book if the current work is part of a series, for reference.

Design and layout for fiction is usually fairly simple: one-color text, chapter heads and/or titles, date and place lines, paragraphs of body text (but also sometimes letters, excerpts, text messages, and so on), ornaments and space breaks between sections. Proofreading fiction requires an even lighter hand than copyediting—fixing outright errors only and querying anything else that appears incorrect—because corrections are more expensive and time-consuming at this stage. In addition to reading the text, the proofreader also checks the layout and typography for correct use of fonts, proper word breaks, widows and orphans, and so on.

See *CMOS* for information about the mechanics of proofreading. Louise Harnby's website (see the Recommended Resources) is also a rich resource for fiction proofreaders.

Part II

Building Your Fiction Style Sheet

An important part of the copyeditor's job is to compile a style sheet for each manuscript. A good fiction style sheet contains not only style information such as treatment of spelling, grammar and usage, punctuation, numbers, and abbreviations but also details about the characters and places mentioned in the story and the timeline and plot. Most publishers require copyeditors to create a style sheet; indie authors can also use your style sheet as a reference. If a style sheet is available from a previous book by that author or a previous book in the series, use that as your starting point. (See chapter 2 for more on reviewing previous style sheets.)

I maintain each fiction style sheet as four documents (general style, characters, places, and timeline) for ease of navigation (see Appendix B: File Management). You might combine these sections into one document while you are working, with bookmarks to take you to each section quickly. Or you can keep them separate and combine them into one document when the edit is finished. Over the next four chapters, I discuss these sections of a fiction style sheet in more detail.

This book functions as a fiction-oriented supplement to *The Chicago Manual of Style* (although it is *not* intended to be a style manual in and of itself). General style manuals such as *CMOS* are geared toward nonfiction; although much of the advice they offer can be applied to fiction (within the story itself, as well as in supplemental material such as endnotes or a "Further Reading" list for a historical novel), applying a rigid style across every work of fiction would be a mistake. The chapters in part II provide a guide to making style choices that are appropriate to each fiction manuscript, even if (or perhaps *particularly when*) they differ from *CMOS*.

3

General Style

How do you decide what to include in the general style section of your fiction style sheet? As noted previously, style manuals such as *CMOS* are geared toward nonfiction; they provide a good starting point for many style issues, but in fiction, appropriate choices may differ from what your style manual recommends. It's fine to break from *CMOS* or even your dictionary if the author's style or the character's voice calls for it or if doing so serves the story. Let's look at some examples:

- Include anything that could be treated in more than one way: For height, is it *six foot two* or *six-two*, both, or neither? With or without hyphens? *Oh yeah* or *oh, yeah*? *Facade* or *façade*? Are words used as words set in italics (the word *hefty*) or roman in quotes (the word "hefty")?
- Add anything that you had to look up; if you had to look it up, someone else might want to as well. Put it on the style sheet and save them the trouble.
- Ask yourself: Is this term or decision likely to come up in a subsequent book, if this is a series? For example, the first book in a series about dragons might contain many instances of the word *wingspan*; is it one word or two? *MW11* spells it as one word, so no decision is needed—but record it on the style sheet for future reference. The next copyeditor will thank you.
- For books in a series, carry over any "(series style)" or "(au pref)" decisions that appear on previous style

sheets or that are communicated to you for the first book in a
series.

- At the same time, you don't need to go overboard. You
  can often cover a whole category by listing a few examples
  together:

a red dragon, a blue dragon; the Reds, the Blues
hit play; the record button

- Consider the audience of your style sheet: a first-time author,
  an author whose first language is not English, or a client who
  is not a publisher may need more detailed documentation and
  explanation for style choices.
- Label on your style sheet any entries that were queried in the
  manuscript, so future users know that there's a question that
  needs an answer. You might highlight the text, or insert a code
  such as (?) after it (I put this in bold with yellow highlighting,
  for extra visibility); add a note at the top of the style sheet
  explaining what your notation means.

(?) = queried in ms. (at the top of the style sheet)
the Grand [High](?) Mage (in the body of the style sheet)

The examples given in this chapter and throughout this book are
not a rigid style guide; they are suggestions of different ways to handle each issue, consistent with the needs of fiction and often different
from what would be recommended in *CMOS* or other general style
guides. Publisher house style and author preferences vary. Occasionally the copyeditor is instructed to follow the author's style even if it's
inconsistent; maybe a comma is used in *oh, sure* and *oh, boy* but not
in *oh yes* and *oh no*. This is fine. Really! It's their book and their style.
Simply record the decision on the style sheet.

If you find yourself waffling over a style decision that isn't covered
by your reference sources, and the author or publisher has no preference, pick something that makes sense for the context. There may
not be a reference for your choice, and that's okay. In fiction, we often
have to make up our own rules.

Figure 3.1 at the end of the chapter illustrates examples of entries
for general style. A fiction style sheet usually includes sections on

numbers, punctuation, typography, abbreviations, usage, miscellaneous topics that don't fit elsewhere, and a word list. Let's discuss these categories in detail.

Numbers

Numbers in fiction are usually spelled out, especially in dialogue, but there are exceptions. For example, phone numbers (particularly *911*, the emergency number in the United States), years (*back in 1865*), decimals, vehicle model numbers and call signs (*Ford F-150, Snake 903*), and weapon names and calibers (*AK-47, .22-caliber*) are usually presented in digits. Another example is numbers that are written on paper, lit up on a screen, painted on a sign, and so on (*The bank's sign flashed 4:05 a.m.*). In general, use digits for numbers that would become unwieldy if spelled out (such as precise money amounts: *$765.04*) and for numbers that are commonly recognized as digits and would be difficult to parse if spelled out (*9/11, 5G*), even in dialogue.

Let's look at some specific examples that you're likely to encounter.

NUMBERS IN DIALOGUE

The traditional rule is to spell out numbers in dialogue, but the trend is moving toward using digits in some cases, especially when spelling a number out would be clunky. However, representing a number in words is useful to show how a character is saying a number: *350* could be spoken as *three-fifty, three hundred fifty,* or *three hundred and fifty.* (See chapter 8 for a more extensive discussion of numbers in dialogue.)

TIME

Hours: Expressions of time are generally spelled out in both narration and dialogue, unless they are precise times (5:37 p.m.) or digital clock displays. (However, an exception to this might make sense if only a few exact times appear throughout, so that they would stand out if expressed in digits. Also consider whether a bunch of precise times are tightly clustered; in that case, digits would make more sense.) Most publishers spell out whole hours and quarter-hour increments: one o'clock, six thirty. *CMOS* omits the hyphen between hours and minutes (two forty-five); one of my publisher clients prefers a hyphen there (four-thirty, seven-forty-five), so I have flagged that entry on that client's style sheet template as ([Client] house style) to show that it's a deliberate choice.

AM/PM: CMOS style allows for either lowercase with periods (a.m./p.m.) or small caps, with or without periods (A.M./P.M., AM/ PM); fiction authors tend to choose lowercase. If a preference isn't given, your first pass will reveal the prevailing style, if one exists.

Some authors use words, not digits, with these abbreviations, especially with whole hours (five a.m. instead of 5:00 a.m.). Let the context be your guide: is a character waking up at five a.m. as a roundish number, or does the train leave at exactly 1:00 p.m.? If there is variation, record the differences.

Military time: Expressions of military time are generally also spelled out in narration and dialogue (fourteen hundred hours, oh seven hundred). However, there are exceptions, such as in date lines (Andrews Air Force Base, 2100 hours) or if a lot of times are clustered close together.

DAYS/YEARS/DECADES

Month and day: Month-and-day dates are usually written as digits in narration (August 4, 4 August) and spelled out in dialogue (August fourth, the fourth of August). But exceptions abound. Some authors prefer to keep digits in dialogue. Digits also may be a better choice in dialogue if many dates are tightly clustered, if the character is quoting something that's written as digits, and so on. A classic example: 9/11—referring to the terrorist attacks on September 11, 2001—is most easily understood as digits.

Digits for dates are also commonly used in date lines in chapter heads (Sunday, June 4, 2017), salutations in written letters, computer text such as email and text message headers (12/16/2020, 4:55 PM), and the like. If it would be in digits in the format that's being represented, it should stay that way.

Years: Years are usually styled as digits (1976) in both narration and dialogue. *CMOS* recommends recasting if a year appears at the beginning of a sentence—and some years are awkward to spell out, because readers must pause to parse the words as referring to a year (The year 2020 was one for the history books! instead of Twenty twenty was one for the history books!).

Occasionally the year is truncated (the class of '68, back in aught-five). (Note that aught-five is spelled out as an expression of the character's voice.) The apostrophe is necessary if digits are used; verify that it's not an open single quote mark ('68).

Decades: Decades may be spelled out (the seventies) or rendered as digits (the 1980s, an '80s movie), although spelled out seems to be slightly more common. As with truncated years, ensure that the apostrophe is set correctly.

HEIGHT

Heights are generally spelled out (five foot nothing; five feet, six inches tall; six-six). An exception would be if they are given as digits on a form (Height: 5′7″; make sure those are foot and inch marks, not single and double quotation marks, and that the use of a space between feet and inches is consistent if there's more than one instance) or in a text message, for example. Either feet or foot may be used for voice in the construction five feet three. Hyphenate the adjective form before a noun (he was a six-foot-two hunk), but leave the hyphens out everywhere else (he stood six foot two).

AGES

Terms involving ages are often improperly hyphenated; if this happens, it's a good idea to record any examples that occur.

    a forty-five-year-old woman
    he is three months old
    my six-year-old is learning to read

CLOTHING/SHOE SIZES

Whole-number clothing and shoe sizes can generally be spelled out (size eight). If the size is shown on a tag or contains a fraction, digits may be a better choice (she wore a 7½ narrow).

ROOM NUMBERS

Treatment of room numbers varies, depending on context. Is the number part of the official name of the room, on a plaque next to the door, and thus similar to a proper name (Conference Room 3)? Is it just the number on the door, as for a hotel room, and thus a simple common noun (room 1138, treatment room one)? Should the adjoining words be capped or lowercased? Consider the context and prevailing style.

ADDRESSES AND STREET/HIGHWAY NUMBERS

CMOS gives good guidance for addresses and street and highway numbers. Because digits are traditional for house numbers and numbered highways, they are easier to parse in both narration and dialogue (12 Royal Ave., No. 4 Primrose Lane, Route 66, I-90); however, exceptions exist (One World Trade Center). Also consider how frequently and how tightly clustered such numbers appear. Record whether terms like *Street* and *Boulevard* are spelled out and how they are treated in newspaper articles, on envelopes, on signs, and so on.

Numbered streets generally follow *CMOS* (Forty-Fifth Street, 125th Street); however, if the story is set in Manhattan and there are a lot of references to streets and avenues, a common choice is words for the avenues (Fifth Avenue) and numbers for the streets (42nd Street, 110th Street).

Punctuation

Oh boy! Punctuation can be tricky. Some rules are fairly strict, such as the traditional rules for delineating dialogue (see chapter 8), because they provide signposts for the reader.[1] But punctuation is often a creative choice, and as long as that choice doesn't cause confusion, the wise copyeditor leaves it alone or polishes it very lightly. Although many punctuation conventions aid the reader and should be preserved, authors often deliberately break punctuation rules to create pacing, mood, dialect, and other effects. Publishers often ask

---

1. Most of the time, traditional rules for punctuating dialogue prevail, but occasionally authors get inventive, and as long as the system makes sense in context, it's fine for authors to use a creative approach—and for copyeditors to edit it according to its own rules. See Carol Saller's article "When Characters Speak: Formatting Dialogue" at the *CMOS Shop Talk* blog for more information.

the copyeditor to leave the author's comma choices unless they create confusion or an egregious error. Tread carefully! Let's look at some examples.

INDIVIDUAL PUNCTUATION MARKS

The following sections discuss some of the most common issues in fiction regarding particular punctuation marks and their use. Punctuation for dialogue is covered in detail in chapter 8.

THE SERIAL COMMA

Most authors use the *serial comma* or *Oxford comma* (as recommended by *CMOS*), but some prefer to omit it. If the publisher approves that choice, record it on the style sheet as (au pref). Maybe even highlight it, since it's an unusual choice. And if your brain works like mine and you might miss any serial commas that sneaked in and shouldn't be there, run a quick search-and-replace to highlight all instances of ", and" and ", or" (*and* or *or* preceded by a comma and a space) so you can check each one as you edit. Some will be false positives, such as coordinating conjunctions joining two independent clauses. But you may be surprised by how many errant serial commas you catch.

THE "SPOUSAL COMMA"

Traditional punctuation rules state that a name used as an appositive must be set off with commas if it is nonrestrictive: *His wife, Raza, had served the empire longer than he had.* However, this rule can be relaxed in fiction, especially when many instances of the "spousal comma" would occur close together and the relationship is clear: *My son Max, his dog Spike, and my husband Jonathan were waiting outside.* The narrator has only one son, granddog, and husband, but the reader knows that, and inserting a bunch of commas and semicolons would add much distraction and little benefit.

COMMAS AROUND *TOO, EITHER, ANYWAY,* AND OTHER ADVERBS

Some authors and publishers are particular about whether certain adverbs are set off by commas, and in what position in the sentence (often designated as *internal* or *terminal*). *Too* and *either* are the most common examples, but *anyway, as well, though, now,* and *then* also get their turn. The chosen style may be to use or not use commas with some or all of these terms, in various positions or as different parts of speech, or not specified at all. Here are some examples where commas may or may not be included:

> I love you too. (no comma before terminal *too*)
> He wondered, too, if she had simply forgotten. (commas around internal *too*)
> Me, either!
> What difference does it make, anyway?
> She poured me a cup as well.
> I don't think he saw me, though.
> Now, cut that out! (*now* as interjection)
> Now he just wanted to go home. (*now* as adverb)
> OK then!

If these choices are already specified from a previous style sheet, retain them. Otherwise, assume that comma placement is the author's choice in each instance and stet (unless it is egregiously, undeniably incorrect). An exception might be if, for example, all instances but one of "Me too!" (or a similar short phrase) omit the comma; for consistency's sake it might be good to delete that one stray comma.

COMMA SPLICES

Comma splices are frequently allowed in fiction, particularly in dialogue, for pacing and other dramatic effects and simply to reflect how people think and talk. Generally, unless there is a stated prohibition against them, it's fine to allow them and add a note to the punctuation section of the style sheet. If a manuscript contains only one or two comma splices, you may wish to query the author about them, in case they were unintentional.

SEMICOLONS

Some authors (and some publishers) specify "no semicolons," on the grounds that that they are too formal for fiction, especially dialogue. This can be true to a point (for example, they are seldom used in YA fiction), but they have their uses. Regardless, if the author or publisher has stated this preference, add it to the style sheet (noting "au pref" or "house style") and follow it. And just as when the serial comma is being omitted, it's a good idea to run a search for semicolons after the edit to make sure you didn't miss any.

ELLIPSES

Use of the three-dot ellipsis only, even following a complete sentence, is most common in fiction, but some authors use four dots if the house style allows for it. Record the style for ellipses either way. Some publishers prefer to use the Word ellipsis character; others use spaced periods, with or without nonbreaking spaces to keep the symbol on one line. Applying this preference should be part of your cleanup routine before you begin the edit.

INTERROBANGS

The interrobang can be rendered as either a single symbol (‽) or as a double mark (*!?* or *?!*). Most publishers either prohibit it, limit its use, or require the use of either *?* or *!* but not both. However, it tends to be more permissible in writing with an extremely light and casual tone, such as YA fiction.

GENERAL PUNCTUATION EXAMPLES

The punctuation section is also a good place to record generic examples of punctuation style choices, instead of putting a specific term in the alphabetical word list. For example, fifth-grader (n) goes here instead of under *F* in the general word list, because it shows how this *type* of term is treated instead of this *specific* word. (Why would someone go to the *F* section of the word list to look up how to treat the grade a student is in? It's a punctuation issue; illustrating the general rule here makes it much easier to find compared to skimming the word list looking for specific terms.) Other examples include global treatment of prefixes and suffixes (half-, -sized, -looking), categories of compound adjectives (late-evening and early-afternoon, Spanish-language, second-largest) and examples of en dash use (World War II–era, Snoop Dogg–like). Let's look at some other common categories particular to fiction.

COLOR TERMS

The hyphenation table in *CMOS* is a good place to start—but some authors prefer a more open punctuation style (a sea green dress rather than a sea-green dress). Some distinguish between terms that are an example of the color and those that are merely a source of reference for the color; for example, sky-blue walls are the color of the sky, but a navy blue jacket is not the color of the navy. *Dark* and *light* color terms are generally left open (dark brown eyes). Watch for terms that change meaning if the hyphen is omitted: dirty-blond hair is a specific color, whereas dirty blond hair is blond hair that needs washing; a muddy-brown car and a muddy brown car are two different things. Generally, unless you have been given specific preferences from a previous book, it's safe to follow *CMOS*.

PHRASAL ADJECTIVES

Preferences often vary for treatment of phrasal adjectives (a deer-in-the-headlights expression). Should they be roman and hyphenated, as in the previous sentence? Roman in quotes, without hyphens (a "deer in the headlights" expression)? Italic (a *deer in the headlights* expression), with or without hyphens? Maybe even just roman, no special treatment, if there's no chance of misreading. Is the phrase a complete sentence (the place had a real "you're very likely to get killed in here" vibe)? Is it a gesture or look standing in for speech (I was quite familiar with her "you're in a lot of trouble" posture)? Some authors prefer to treat all of these categories differently.

When the author or publisher has not specified a preference, it seems simplest to stick with roman and hyphenated, as in the first example. Hyphens tie the expression together as a unit, and use of quotation marks can look cluttered or suggest speech where it's not intended. Italics can work well too.

EXCLAMATIONS

Introductory exclamations such as *oh* or *ah* are often followed by a comma, especially if they are followed by a name or a phrase (Oh, Emily, what will we do?; Ah, the splendor of youth). But the author may omit the comma if the expression is a short, common phrase (Oh boy, Oh God, Oh no!) or for pacing or voice. Record specific examples so you can compare them. You can also run a search for *oh* and *ah* after the edit to review all examples at once, keeping in mind that the author may choose to use or omit the comma on a case-by-case basis. If there's no clear deliberate style, it's fine to leave the inconsistency. (See chapter 8 for more examples.)

STUTTERING AND HESITATION IN DIALOGUE

Stuttering is usually indicated with hyphens between repeated sounds or words (I-I-I don't know what you mean; She b-b-broke her p-promise!); some authors and publishers prefer em dashes between complete words (You—you—you monster!). When a stuttered sound is a digraph, repeat both letters to represent the repeated sound (Th-there it is!; Sh-sh-should I stay?). Note that the capital letter is not repeated at the beginning of a sentence, but do repeat it if the word is a proper noun (Wh-where is G-Grandma?).

Hesitation, on the other hand, calls for an ellipsis (Did . . . did I hurt you?). Generally the first word after the ellipsis is capped if it starts a new sentence and lowercased if it does not.

See chapter 8 for more examples of how to handle various forms of broken-up words and sentences in dialogue.

POSSESSIVES OF NAMES ENDING IN -S, -X, ETC.

Always include a line about possessives of names ending in *-s* or *-x* or *-z* and whether to include the *s* after the apostrophe. Most of the time, the answer is yes, in accordance with *CMOS*; the advantage of always appending *'s* is that it's consistent and requires no decision. However, some authors prefer apostrophe-only for such names (Chris', Buzz'). It's a legitimate choice, even if it's contrary to *CMOS* style, so if the publisher approves, record it on the style sheet, labeled with the "(au pref)" tag.

Watch out for awkward plural possessives of names ending in *-s* (the Sanderses' house). Some authors get these wrong at first (the Adam's house or the Adams's house, referring to the house that belongs to the Adams family). Even though *the Adamses' house* is correct, it will look odd to some readers, who may stop to figure out whether it's right and be drawn out of the story. If *Adamses'* appears only one or two times, it's probably fine; if it's more frequent, that may be less fine. Sometimes simply changing the phrase from possessive to attributive form (*the Adams house*) does the trick. If not, it may help to add a query explaining that you've changed it to the correct form, but that readers may still find it distracting, and asking the author to consider choosing a different name to eliminate the problem.

Typography (roman/italic/capitalization)

Fiction contains many elements that are rare in nonfiction. Direct thought, indirect thought, imagined dialogue, mouthed dialogue, remembered speech, telepathic dialogue, words as words or sounds, letters as letters or shapes or academic grades, signs, words on clothing, handwriting, text messages, emails, typed text, computer commands: these can be treated in many different ways. Italics? Small caps? Caps and small caps? A Word character style defined by the publisher or designer just for that element (such as "computer text")? Roman in quotation marks? All caps? Initial caps? Title case? It all goes in the typography section of your style sheet.

You may be tempted to try to devise a different treatment for each type of expression to help readers tell them apart; however, you don't want the text to look like a ransom note either. Context goes a long way toward conveying what type of communication is being represented. Keep it simple!

ORGANIZING ENTRIES

I recommend not grouping entries in this section under headings like "Roman," "Italic," "Small Caps," and so on. If someone needs to look up how words used as words are treated, they'll be looking for *words as words*, not *things that are italic*. (The dictionary isn't sorted into nouns, verbs, adjectives, and so on!) Help them out and organize by category: types of dialogue, words as words/sounds, letters as letters/sounds/shapes, written/printed text, electronic communication, terms of address, non-English language, and so on. Organizing things this way also helps you see how similar items are treated if you need to make a decision.

Let's look at some common examples. Author and house style will be your main guides, and they vary; the examples given here, which are generally the most common style choices, are suggestions if no preference is given.

Styling spoken dialogue the traditional way is easy: roman text in quotation marks (with italics for emphasis as needed).[2] Recent discussions about disability include sign language in this category when it is the character's customary way of speaking. Context can convey (if necessary) that sign language is being used (for example, the narration may say that the character is deaf or describe her angry hand motions). Deaf people disagree on the most appropriate way to represent signed speech; one accepted option is to put it in quotation marks just like spoken words. (See Laura Brown's blog post on writing ASL at disabilityinkidlit.com for a thoughtful analysis.) Either *said* or *signed* is an appropriate dialogue tag.

Next we consider "not spoken" exchanges: thoughts, imagined or remembered dialogue, telepathic communication, and so on. Generally these are set in italics, to identify them to the reader and to avoid sprinkling quotation marks all over the manuscript and possibly confusing actual speech with not-really-speech. Let's look at some common examples (see also chapter 8):

- *Direct thought* (words that a character is actually thinking; usually in present tense): *I wish I had never gone to Paris.* Usually set in italics, though some authors prefer roman; stet roman if it is clearly a deliberate choice.
- *Indirect thought* (a description of what a character is thinking): She wished she had never gone to Paris. Always roman (though it may include italics for emphasis as needed), because it's really narration describing the person's thoughts.
- *Imagined dialogue:* Fluffy meowed as if to say *Feed me!* Usually italic; some authors prefer roman in quotes. I suggest that using italics helps convey that it's not actually being

2. But see also the footnote earlier in this chapter regarding alternative methods of presenting dialogue.

spoken. (See also the section titled "When 'Dialogue' Isn't Dialogue" in chapter 8.)

- *Mouthed dialogue:* I glanced over and mouthed, *Really?* Similar to imagined dialogue; here also, using italics supports its not-spoken nature.
- *Remembered dialogue:* She thought back to his last words before he left: *Don't come looking for me.* Also similar to imagined dialogue. Usually italic; sometimes roman in quotes or italic in quotes. (See the section titled "Action bloopers" in chapter 9 for more information about remembered dialogue.)
- *Telepathic dialogue: Where have you been?* Her voice was frantic in my mind. Similar to direct thought, except that it's being directed toward another character. Usually italic, though an author might choose roman in quotes and let context convey the telepathy, or sometimes italic in quotes.
- *Flashbacks:* Brief flashbacks, no longer than a paragraph or two, may work in italics. However, longer passages can be tiring to read if they are entirely in italics; it may be better to set them roman, with space breaks and/or transition text before and after (a query to the author may be needed).

WORDS, LETTERS, SOUNDS, AND SHAPES

CMOS is pretty much spot-on for treatment of words as words, letters as letters, and so on in fiction. Let's review here.

- *Words as words:* the word *bumfuzzled.* Per *CMOS,* usually italic, but roman in quotes is an equally valid alternative. This is one of the entries that always goes on my style sheet.
- *Words as sounds:* the *clank-clunk* of his walker. Preferences vary for whether and when to use italics for sounds. Some publishers specify italics only for words not in the house dictionary (*mmph*). Sounds used as verbs are often partly italicized (she *tsk*ed). Sometimes italics for sounds are applied case by case, such as for emphasis or simply according to author preference—or not at all.
- *Letters as letters:* the envelope marked with a *B.* Per *CMOS,* usually italic; a few common expressions are exceptions (mind

your p's and q's; dot the i's and cross the t's). Follow *CMOS* for plurals of letters: a roman letter plus *s* for capital letters (the three Rs) and an italic letter plus roman *'s* for lowercase, to avoid misreading (two *i*'s).

- *Letters as sounds:* a twanging of his *a*'s. Usually italic and lowercase.
- *Letters as shapes:* His mouth formed an O; the buildings formed a U shape. Usually cap and roman, in the normal body text font. (The older style of using a sans serif font for letters as shapes is outdated; the sans serif doesn't do more to convey the shape, and it can look awkward.)
- *Letters as grades:* I got an A on my history test! Her grades were mostly Bs and Cs. *CMOS* prevails here as well: cap and roman, with no apostrophe for plurals.

WRITTEN AND PRINTED TEXT

Words that exist as written material in the story can be represented in a variety of ways. Add specific examples from the manuscript to your style sheet.

Some of the examples that follow mention Word character styles; some publishers specify a character style for certain elements, so that they appear in a different font altogether. For these you will apply the style (if it's not already applied) by selecting the text and then selecting the character style from the Styles dialog, instead of applying a manual font attribute such as italics or small caps.

- *Signs, labels, and inscriptions:* a No Smoking sign. Signs may be in italics, quotes, or a Word character style, and may also be in all caps or title case, small caps or roman. In some manuscripts, short standard signs (a For Sale sign) get no special treatment other than title case, whereas a longer sign might be in italics, small caps, or a Word character style (a rusty sign announcing that TRESPASSERS WILL BE SHOT—SURVIVORS WILL BE SHOT AGAIN). Plentiful examples pulled from the manuscript to the style sheet will help you decide how to treat different cases if no preference is given.
- *Headlines:* There it was, right on the front page: *Four Dead in*

Freak Accident. As for signs and inscriptions, treatment varies widely; the only difference is that Word character styles are less commonly used.

- *Words on clothing:* Their ratty hoodie was emblazoned with WHIRLED PEAS on the front. The treatment of words on clothing is similar to that of signs, inscriptions, and headlines; Word character styles are less common. Capitalization choices may reflect the actual lettering on the clothing (Her pink bedazzled GIRL Power! top twinkled in the sunlight). Note the difference between a shirt that read DOGS RULE (actual words on the shirt) and his Rolling Stones T-shirt (mere description).

- *Handwritten or typed text:* I scribbled Moe's Bar, 10 pm on a napkin. Usually italic, but some authors prefer roman in quotes. (Note that stylistic consistency is not necessary here; handwriting and other "organic" text does not have to conform to the overall style. Here, *10 pm* is what the person wrote, regardless of the style for time on your style sheet.)

- *Letters: My darling Kirk,* he wrote . . . Similar to handwriting. Occasionally a Word character style using a handwriting font is specified as a design choice.

- *Text being read aloud:* I began reading the letter. "'Dear Lily, I'm sorry that I had to leave so suddenly . . .'" Usually treated as a quote within a quote, with single quotes inside double quotes in US style, or the reverse in UK style. Occasionally italics are used. Make sure that all nested quote marks are turned the right way.

COMPUTER TEXT AND ELECTRONIC COMMUNICATION AND DEVICES

Electronic communication has become a large part of our lives, and thus also a large part of our literature. Here as in other categories, examples from the manuscript illustrate previous style decisions and inform new ones.

- *Text messages:* My phone vibrated. *Are you ok? Call me.* Text messages are usually set in italics or in a Word character style, often a monospaced "computer" font like Courier New to convey the electronic nature of the text. (However, in self-publishing and especially ebook formatting, it's often safer to stick to standard fonts as much as possible.) Also note that text messages are casual writing and often don't follow formal spelling, capitalization, and punctuation rules.

- *Emails:* Hi Drake, he read. *We received the files and were able to open them* . . . Similar to text messages, email text is usually rendered in italics or (less often) a "computer" font. If email addresses that could be real are shown, query the author to confirm that they are fictionalized or reserved (see chapter 9).
- *Internet search terms:* When she googled "great white shark attacks Australia," the results were no help. Internet searches and other text typed online is usually set roman in quotes, in italics, or (rarely) in a "computer" font.
- *Text on screens:* The display changed to NO SIGNAL. Screens can include computers, phones, TVs, car dashboards, aircraft and spaceship controls, and any electronic device. All caps, small caps, caps and small caps, roman in quotes, italics, Word character style: all are possible choices. It just depends what's on the screen and how it's best represented. Different types of displays may be treated differently; if there are a lot of them, put plenty of illustrative examples on the style sheet.
- *Buttons and controls:* She tapped Send and closed the window. Buttons and controls can be physical (an actual button that you *push* or *press*) or virtual (an image on a screen that you *tap* or *click*), and they can be generic (Jordan hit play) or specific (It seemed to take forever to locate the WARP DRIVE lever). The text can also specify the actual label on a control (I glanced at the EXEC switch) or describe the function on an unlabeled control (He angrily punched the Talk button). These are almost always roman; lowercase is commonly used for more general usage and initial caps or all caps for specific functions and labels.

These are only a few examples of technical devices you might encounter; consistency is key, along with examples on the style sheet to illustrate different choices for different situations.

NON-ENGLISH TERMS

In fiction, non-English terms may be in real languages or invented languages. For real languages, the traditional treatment has been to set in italics any non-English words that do not appear in the house dictionary (so if you are using *MW11*, you would italicize *buon giorno* but not "a cappella"). Alternatively, and especially in nonfiction, such terms are sometimes italicized on first use only. However, as publishers, editors, and authors seek to embrace inclusive language, there is a growing movement to set all non-English terms roman, to avoid *othering* them (treating them as foreign, different, or separate). This is a valid consideration; however, an argument for retaining italics for non-English terms is that it provides a cue to readers who are not fluent in English, have reading disorders, or otherwise need a hint that the word is not English and thus not one that they would be expected to recognize. If the chosen style is not clear, consult with the author or publisher before starting the edit.

In fiction, and especially in fantasy and other fiction set in invented worlds, another consideration is whether the term is a part of the language or culture of the setting. Invented worlds often include rich invented languages that are woven throughout the characters' everyday speech and action. If we know (through either context or definition) that a harziik is a sword, the word doesn't need to be italicized throughout, and setting the invented language of the story in roman helps with the suspension of disbelief. Just an ordinary word, everyone knows what this is, carry on!

However, in an invented world, the author may *intend* to "other" a foreign language for the purpose of the story, to emphasize that a speaker, object, or concept does not belong to the dominant society. Or, for example, the rules of the invented society may call for certain terms such as honorifics to be italicized. I have even been asked (per the author's preference) to ensure that in a fantasy story that featured two countries, words from each country's language were roman when spoken in that country or by a native speaker, and italic when spoken outside that country by a non-native speaker. In addition, people from both countries regularly traveled back and forth. (This required a separate full pass!) This is one area where your first pass through the manuscript will give you a clue as to the author's intent and style, so you can follow it accordingly during the second pass (or query before proceeding if it's not clear).

There are always exceptions, such as when the word is being emphasized (*"Merde!* It's locked!") or for a word used as a word (He reserves *ma chérie* for me). A word that's used only once, in a sense where the intent is to present it as foreign or unusual, is another case where italics might be appropriate. Consider frequency of use and context, and query when in doubt.

See chapter 8 for examples of how to handle non-English dialogue that is followed by a translation to assist the reader.

WORDS AND NAMES FOR PEOPLE

Capitalization rules for all the various ways to address and refer to people other than by their proper names can be tricky. Let's look at some of them.

- *Terms of endearment (and those not so dear):* sweetheart, pumpkin, my dear, ma'am, jerkface. Generic terms used to address someone that are not an established nickname for that person are lowercased. A useful test for endearments is this: Would someone refer to that person by that term when talking to someone else? ("The other day Sunshine said . . .") If yes, it's a nickname and should be capped. If not, it's generic and lowercased. There will always be exceptions, of course, but most cases will follow this pattern.
- *Occupational titles used in place of a name:* Yes, Doctor; Why did you stop me, Officer?; Stand down, Lieutenant! Usually capped. However, words that also function as a generic noun that describes the person and are used less formally can be lowercased (It really hurts, doc!; Excuse me, waiter).
- *Civil, religious, and military titles:* the president, the ambassador, the Emperor; the archbishop; the colonel, the Director. Usually lowercased. However, as illustrated in these examples, such terms are sometimes capped, especially in speculative and historical fiction, to emphasize the importance of particular personages, per author's voice. Also,

when referring to the FBI, the Director and the Bureau are traditionally capped.

- *Titles of nobility and other honorifics:* Your Honor, Her Grace, His Majesty. Often capped both in address and when used to refer to the person indirectly. Titles involving the words *lord* and *lady* are frequently lowercased (my lord, m'lady, your ladyship). See KJ Charles's blog post on nobility titles (listed in the Recommended Resources) for an excellent overview.

- *Temporary epithets:* Mr. Wonderful, Miss High-and-Mighty, Cowboy Guy. Usually capped because they are taking the place of a name.

- *Familial terms:* Mom, Daddy, Uncle Cho, Gran. Capped in direct address (You're embarrassing me, Mom!) and when used as a name (What did Mom say?) but not when used as a common noun (My mom is so weird). Note that *Aunt Sadie* is her name, but she is *my aunt Sadie.* Also pay attention to consistency in spelling: is it *Papa, Pops,* or *Pop-Pop? Grandad* or *Granddad?* Make it consistent (being mindful of whether different characters are using different voices), and record it on your style sheet.

- Exceptions to capping familial terms in address include terms like *sister/sis, brother/bro, cousin/cuz,* and *grandpa/grandma,* especially when the person is not actually a relative (You and me both, sister! Get out of the way, grandpa!).

RELIGIOUS TERMS

CMOS prescribes lowercasing pronouns referring to the Abrahamic deity (Jesus and his flock), and this logically extends to other terms: the devil, heaven, hell, purgatory, paradise, sign of the cross, mass. However, if the work has a strong religious theme, the author may prefer to cap such terms.

Ensure that terms relating to any religion, real or invented, are treated consistently and accurately with regard to spelling and capitalization. If there are a lot of them, it may help to group them as a category on your style sheet. See also the section titled "Conscious language" in chapter 7.

ASTRONOMICAL TERMS

Generally, terms like *sun, moon, earth,* and *universe* can be lowercased, unless the author has capped them for a more mystical feel. Some authors distinguish *Earth* (the planet) from *earth* (soil). Lowercase *earth* in adjective forms and generic expressions: earthly, what on earth, down to earth.

MISCELLANEOUS CAPITALIZATION CHOICES

Each manuscript has its own variety of terms that need a decision about capitalization and other style choices. The following examples are not style prescriptions, but just a few categories of terms that you'll need to decide how to style as you copyedit.

plan B
shift into park
say yes, a firm no
waypoint Alpha
department names: Ballistics, Internal Affairs
Gray Team
he pronounced it as *Fronch*

Abbreviations, acronyms, and initialisms

Abbreviations (for simplicity, let's use one term to encompass all three types) used in a novel might be real (GPS, FYI) or invented ones from the story's fictional world, such as names of organizations (PRT for Paranormal Response Team) or fictional technology. Include real abbreviations with their spelled-out forms in your list, whether they have been spelled out or not, simply to clarify what they stand for. For fictional abbreviations, list the spelled-out version to catch inconsistencies. Unlike in nonfiction, there is no need to spell out abbreviations on first use, as in a textbook; rather, let the narration and dialogue explain them naturally for the reader, and query if they are not clear from context.

Usage

Authors and publishers may specify usage preferences to be applied in narration, dialogue (depending on character voice), or both. First-person point of view is usually treated similarly to dialogue because it's also the voice of that character. (See chapter 8 for a more extensive discussion.)

The following are examples of typical usage notes:

distinguish between that/which, further/farther, each other/one
    another (often with an explanation of the usage rule)
use of dialogue tags that aren't verbs of utterance (see
    chapter 8)
allow misplaced *both/only/either* in dialogue
allow sentence fragments
most important/most importantly

See the Recommended Resources for a list of usage guides.

Miscellaneous

Ah, "Miscellaneous," the junk drawer of the style sheet. This section of your style sheet is the home of style decisions and notes about terms and categories, real and fictional, that don't fit elsewhere. The contents of this section vary depending on the contents of the manuscript; various genres have similar entries and lists of items both real and fictional. Here are some examples:

- *Military thrillers and spy novels:* weapons and equipment, vehicles, aircraft, ships, organizations, operations

  field offices: Berlin station, Paris station
  organizations: Operation Full Throttle, Stingray Six
  aircraft: Mi-28 attack helicopter
  weapons: P90 machine gun

- *Speculative fiction (fantasy/paranormal/sci-fi):* names of clans, creatures, weapons, books and publications, fictional months, holidays, events, councils, magical objects, spaceships, historical eras, mottoes

  Clan Willow; the Willow clan; the clan
  Verdon (month; in the spring)
  the Before Times (before the rise of magic)

- *Historical fiction:* organizations, books and publications, ships, events

  the Diamond Club, the club; the Blue Dahlia Society, the
    society
  RMS *Fortuna*; USS *Walke*
  the Cherry Blossom Ball; the ball

- *Contemporary fiction:* websites, blogs, recipe names, TV stations and programs, films, songs, wines, games, events, dog breeds

  wines: merlot, cabernet, pinot grigio; Côtes du Rhône, Veuve
    Clicquot
  the Hilldale Strawberry Festival (held in late June every year)
  games: follow the leader, hide-and-seek, checkers;
    Monopoly, Sorry!

Grouping these entries by category instead of in an alphabetical list helps you locate items that you don't remember (was the council called the High Lords' Chamber or the Chamber of the High Lords or something else?), find inconsistencies (the Land of Five Clans actually has *six* named clans), and see patterns when you need to make a style decision, such as consistent capitalization (the Masters of Stone, the Masters of Wind, the Masters of Fire, but a stone master, a wind master, a fire master). If those councils or clans or masters were listed in a global alphabetical list, you might not see patterns or inconsistencies. However, as an example, a subhead of "Magical Objects" followed by a list of those objects, listed alphabetically, by type (swords, amulets, jewelry), or by whatever method makes sense, is much more useful.

If only a few items occur in a certain category, you may find it easier to put them elsewhere. However, when you're juggling a lot of similar terms, especially invented ones, grouping them together is helpful when you find yourself thinking, "How did I [or the author] treat other things like this?"

For stories set in the real world, it's often useful to distinguish real elements from fictional ones on the style sheet (such as with an asterisk, with a note explaining that starred items are factual and have been fact-checked for accuracy).

Alphabetical word list

The word list is the place for general vocabulary: specific words that someone would look up, as in a dictionary, rather than terms belonging to a category. Part of speech often matters, so list it after each term; here are the most common abbreviations:

adjective: (a) or (adj)
adverb: (adv)
noun: (n)
verb: (v)
predicate adjective: (pa)
singular noun: (sing n)
plural noun: (pl n)
interjection: (interj)
preposition: (prep)
trademark: (tm)

Feel free to add other abbreviations as needed—(masc n), (fem n), (conj)—as well as explanations and clarifications:

long-time (contra MW11, per AU)
re-create (create again)
back atcha (back at you)
a Star (only when referring to one of the deities)
Earth (planet)
earth (soil)
at the weekend (BrE) (meaning "British English")

Of course, not every word needs to go here, but here are some guidelines for choosing entries:

- *Words that you had to look up to verify:* Once you've looked it up, put it on the style sheet so the next person doesn't have to. (Some terms I find tricksy are the *half-*, *heart-*, *light-*, and *cold-* compound adjectives and their friends: *halfhearted, heartbreaking, light-headed, cold-blooded,* and so on. I have to look up the hyphenation every time. I keep a list of these terms [and others] on my desk for easy reference. One of these days I'll remember that *absent-minded* takes a hyphen, and I won't have to check my cheat sheet anymore. And then *Merriam-Webster* will probably close it up.) A subcategory is words that are commonly misspelled, such as *liquefy, rarefy, minuscule, faze,* and *horde.*

- *Words that have variants* (in spelling, hyphenation, capitalization, use of diacritics, and so on): Publishers often specify that the first option in the house dictionary must be used, but still, if it appears in the book, record the choice on the style sheet. If the second option is the author's or publisher's preferred style, add the "(au pref)" or "(house style)" tag as appropriate. Common examples include verb forms like *dreamed/dreamt, leaped/leapt, burned/burnt,* and *kneeled/knelt;* US/UK distinctions like *toward/s, among/st,* and *amid/st;* and (one of my favorite catches) words that look weird without the *e* (whether the dictionary lists that form or not): *tingeing, bingeing, eyeing,* and *dyeing.*
- *Words with prefixes:* Pay special attention to words with prefixes. The general rule is to close them up (no hyphen) unless they're listed with a hyphen in the dictionary. But sometimes this results in ambiguity (*I resent the message*—did I send it again, or did it offend me?) or a failure of the ILF ("it looks funny") test (*cochair*); sometimes authors have their own hyphenation preferences regardless of what the dictionary says, or they invent terms using prefixes, in which case the dictionary won't help. If you are waffling over what to do, it helps to see how other words with the same prefix have been treated: whether the stem begins with the same letter as the end of the prefix, what part of speech it is, and so on. So until you're familiar with the overall style, add those prefixed words to your alphabetical list as examples.
- *Phrasal verbs and tricky prepositions:* Phrasal verbs consist of more than one word, the second of which is often a

preposition; they are often confused with their one-word noun forms. Examples include *work out* (v) vs. *workout* (n), *back up* (v) vs. *backup* (n), and *log in* (v) vs. *login* (n). Also watch out for the distinction between *into* and *in to*, *onto* and *on to*, and so on. (You can *turn yourself into* a frog, but you would *turn yourself in to* the police.)

- *Words that were consistently wrong or treated inconsistently:* Correct the form of the word throughout the manuscript and add it to the style sheet (and perhaps write a query explaining the correction, if appropriate).

- *All invented words:* Invented words might be terms from a fictional world or creative license with real words. Where else would we be able to look them up but on the style sheet? This is an example of how fiction gets more leeway: if the author has verbed a noun or made up a technological or slang term, and it makes sense in context, fits the style and voice, and adds flavor, guess what? It's a word, at least in this manuscript. This includes unconventional plurals, spellings, and capitalizations, which are common in speculative fiction, especially fantasy.

    angel-blush (n, v)
    teleport lock (n)
    draw-ish (v) (in manuscript: *I never knew you could draw-ish*)
    Bambi-eyes (v) (in manuscript: *There she was, trying to Bambi-eyes me into letting her have ice cream for breakfast*)
    accidentally-on-purpose (adv) (in manuscript: *Hope thought about hanging up . . . accidentally-on-purpose* [The hyphens are necessary to create a single term.])
    Seeing (v; magical Sight)
    Wizard, the (capped only for the head Wizard; lc for all others)
    Nordan (sing/pl n), a Nordan warrior (adj)

- *UK variants:* If the manuscript uses UK spellings and/or vocabulary, a general note can cover this, but certain words can go on the list to clarify which one is preferred. You don't need to list every example of obvious UK spelling, such as *flavour*, *centre*, and *realise*, but it's helpful to list spellings that sometimes appear in US English, such as *towards*, *amongst*,

learnt, judgement, and *traveller,* as a reminder that those
choices are intentional and correct (see also chapter 7).

- *Non-English terms:* Add real and invented non-English words
  to your list, in italics if that is the chosen style for that word
  or language; it can help to provide the definition if possible.
  Verify real words if you can, or flag them and query the author
  to do so. If there are a lot of non-English terms, or if there are
  a lot of phrases and sentences, consider putting them in their
  own section.
- *Slang and vulgar terms:* bejeezus, dammit, bitch-slap, asshat.
  Many slang terms and "naughty" words aren't in standard
  dictionaries, or they have multiple variant spellings. Is it
  goddammit or *God damn it*? Is *douchebag* as an insult one
  word or two? You may need to consult a resource such as the
  BuzzFeed Style Guide or Urban Dictionary.
- *Trademarks and brand names (real or fictional):* Band-Aid,
  iPhone, SIG Sauer. Traditional publishers generally honor
  capitalization of trademarks to avoid potential litigation. Fact-
  check real trademarks and brand names carefully and record
  them with the designation "(tm)" to show that they should not
  be changed. Add fictional brand names to ensure consistent
  treatment (Whizz-O-Matic 3000). If there are a lot of fictional
  brand names, consider putting them in their own list. (See
  also chapter 9 for further discussion of trademarks.) Also list
  former trademarks like dumpster (n) and touch-tone (n) for
  clarity.
- *Dialogue forms:* woulda, don'tcha, a'course, idjit, if'n, for gosh
  sakes. Spoken contractions can be styled in different ways.
  Consider how to shorten *what do you*. Is it *whadja, whaddya,
  whatcha,* or something else? The dictionary won't help you!
  Choose a spelling and record it on the style sheet. (See also the
  section titled "Dialect and informal dialogue" in chapter 8.)
- *Sounds and interjections:* rat-a-tat-tat, shh, grrrrr. Words as
  sounds that aren't in the dictionary, whether spoken or not,
  can also vary in spelling and treatment. Should *mmm-hmm*
  always have the same number of *m*'s? (Maybe, maybe not.)
  Uh-huh means yes, but *uh-uh* means no. *Ka-ching!* gets a

hyphen so it doesn't look like a verb. Remove all doubt about how sounds should be treated by recording them on the style sheet.

- *Frequent fliers:* backward, cell phone, internet, mustache, T-shirt. Finally, I find myself always including certain words on every style sheet as soon as I encounter them in the text, no matter which variant is being used. (Alternatively, you could add all of your frequent fliers[3] to your style sheet at the beginning of the edit and confirm them as you go, as described in Appendix A: Style Sheet Templates.) Why? Because whenever they show up, they can go either way. Or maybe that word *should* go one way and not the other. Or I can never remember what version is correct and I always have to look it up, so I always put it on the style sheet. Or we're following US style but the author has chosen an alternative spelling for a cultural or historical flavor. Or the author has been inconsistent and hasn't stated a preference, so I apply my own preference.

You may develop your own list of frequent fliers, and your terms may differ from mine. But I'll give you a sample (a slash divides two options):

acknowledgment/acknowledgement (n) (US/UK)
adrenaline (n)
adviser/advisor (n)
aha (interj)
all right/alright (adv) (*alright* is often deemed acceptable in
    fiction, especially in dialogue)
ambience/ambiance
amid/st (US/UK)
amok/amuck
among/st (US/UK)
back seat (n)/backseat (a)

---

3. This is my pet term for recurring style issues and other things that you'll see a lot. You'll, uh, see it a lot in this book.

backward/s (US/UK; also all of the other -*wards* words:
    upward/s, downward/s, inward/s, etc.)
backyard
banister/bannister
barbecue (as opposed to *BBQ* or *barbeque*)
biceps (sing/pl)
blond (*blond hair* for any gender is the norm [adjective]; *he was
    a tall blond* [noun])
blonde (*she was a beautiful blonde* [noun]; some authors prefer
    blonde hair for female characters [adjective])
bloodred/blood red/blood-red
catalog/catalogue (US/UK)
cell phone (some house styles specify *cellphone*)
chaise longue/lounge
crime scene (a, n)
curtsy/curtsey (and all its verb forms)
damnedest (the first *e* is often missing)
decision-making (a), decision making (n)
doorframe (sometimes *door frame*)
doorjamb
email/e-mail (*MW11* has removed the hyphen in the preferred
    spelling)
facade/façade
god-awful
goddamn/goddamned (sometimes both are used)
godforsaken
goodbye/good-bye (*MW11* has removed the hyphen in the
    preferred spelling)
good night (n), good-night (a) (*a good-night kiss*)
gray/grey (US/UK; some US authors prefer *grey*)
hold on to (*on to* is two words)
impostor/imposter
internet/Internet (the trend is to lowercase)
judgment/judgement (US/UK)
law enforcement (a, n)
log in (v)/login (n)

meat loaf/meatloaf
mic/mike (microphone)
mindset/mind-set (*MW11* has removed the hyphen in the
    preferred spelling)
mustache/moustache (US/UK)
naive/naïve, naiveté/naïveté/naivety/naïvety
okay/OK
omelet/omelette
oohs and aahs, oohing and aahing (is it two *a*'s or two *h*'s?)
résumé (n)
seat belt/seatbelt
snuck (This is an acceptable informal past tense. Really.)
son of a bitch/sonovabitch (n)
sweat pants/sweatpants
to-do list
toward/s (US/UK)
T-shirt (A *T-shirt* is shaped like a capital letter T. A *t-shirt* would
    be pretty uncomfortable. Acceptable variations are *tee shirt*
    and *tee*.)
vise (meaning the clamping tool; not *vice*)
voice mail/voicemail
website, web page, the web
whiskey/whisky (sometimes spelling differs depending on where
    the liquor comes from)
wineglass (it took me far too long to realize that *MW11* styles this
    as one word)
workout (n), work out (v)
X-ray (n), x-ray (v)

Preferred spelling and usage changes constantly. Keep up with
language changes by following editorial resources and organizations
online via their websites, social media, blogs, and email newsletters;
for example, you can follow ACES, EFA, *CMOS* (particularly their
monthly Q&A), and Merriam-Webster on Twitter and Facebook. You
can also join online editorial discussion groups to stay up-to-date on
what other editors are talking about and the resources they find useful. See the Recommended Resources at the back of this book.

Fabulous Author, *Contemporary Series Romance*

Project Manager: Janis Doe   Copyeditor: Amy J. Schneider

(?) = queried in ms.

References

Chicago Manual of Style, 17th edition
Merriam-Webster's Collegiate Dictionary, 11th edition

Numbers

Generally, spell out numbers below 100, round numbers, numbers in dialogue; exceptions follow

ten P.M. (Publisher house style)
six-two; five feet even (height)
'06 (year; oh-six in dialogue)
two thirds (a, n)
room 317
911 (emergency number; digits OK in dialogue)
twenty-something (a)
4×4 truck

Abbreviations

aka   also known as
ASAP   as soon as possible
EMT   emergency medical technician
ID   identification
PBJ   peanut butter and jelly
SUV   sport-utility vehicle
TLC   tender loving care

Punctuation

use serial comma
3-point ellipsis ONLY: space between final word and first point (series style)
always lowercase after a colon (series style)

midnight-blue (a); silver-gray (a, n)
farmers' market
driver's side, passenger side (n)
straight As (school grades)
to-do list
early-morning, late-afternoon (a)

Louis's, Torres's (possessive)

Figure 3.1. Sample style sheet: general style

Typography

direct thought, imagined dialogue italic: *Now I've done it*, he thought.
words as words italic: the word *ambitious*
letters as letters cap, italic: an *X* for his signature
letters as shapes cap, roman: the V of her neckline
written notes italic: he wrote *Always* in the mist on the window
e-mail subject lines and text italic
signs, headlines c/sc: BIG SKY DINER

nicknames: Sunshine, Buck

in address: mister, miss; lady, kid, child; hon, sweetie
               Doctor, Sheriff

pronouns referring to God lc: he, his

he clicked Submit
hit play; punch speed dial
she put her car in park

Usage

distinguish: *that/which: that* is restrictive, no comma / *which* is nonrestrictive, use comma
                farther/further: farther for physical distance / *further* for metaphorical distance
                a while/awhile: a while as a noun / *awhile* meaning "for a while" (series style)

allow sentence fragments
allow misplaced *both/only/either*

Miscellaneous

Pleasantville Gazette (weekly newspaper; comes out Thursday afternoon **(?)**)
Hospitality Monthly (magazine)
Wyoming Cooks! (blog)

western (U.S. region)
the States

the navy
.30-06 (rifle)
Colt .45

the Midsummer Music Festival
the Letters to the Editor column

a Log Cabin quilt, a Lone Star quilt

General Word List

Part of speech follows each word:

a	adjective	pa	predicate adjective
adv	adverb	pl n	plural noun
v	verb	prep	preposition
n	noun	interj	interjection
tm	trademark		

adrenaline (n)
afterward (adv)
axe (n) (au pref)

back door (n)
backdoor (a)
bandanna (n)
barbecue (n)
Bible (n)
blond (a, masc n)
blonde (fem n)
bogeyman (n)

café (n)
caller ID (tm)
catalog (n)
chain-link (a)
chiles (peppers)

damn it (interj)
disc (n)
drive-through (n)
duffel bag (n)
dumpster (n)

Earth (planet)
earth (soil)
email (a, n, v)

fast-food (a)
fess up (v)
first-aid (a)

good night (n)
good-bye (n) (au pref)
good-night (a)
gray (a, n)
Grim Reaper (n)
half dozen (a, n)
half listening (v)

happily-ever-after (n)
harrumph (v)
heaven (n)
hiccupped (v)
howdy-do (n)

ice pack (n)
impostor (n)

jack-in-the-box (n)
jeez (interj)
Jell-O (tm)
jump-start (v)

ketchup (n)
key card (n)

lay low (v)
leaped (v)
look-see (n)

makeup (n)
mason jar (n)
mementos (pl n)
mindset (n)
mmm (interj)
multitasking (a, n)

naïve (a)
name tag (n)
non-negotiable (a)
nosy (a)
number one (a, n)

okay (adv)
online (adv)
outta (out of)
Parmesan cheese (n)
pom-poms (n)
Post-it note (tm)

push-up (n)

re-create (create again)
ring tone (n)

safe-deposit box (n)
smiley face (n)
spit (past tense)
streetlight (n)
superpower (n)

tabby cat (n)
takeout (a, n)
thank-you note (n)
thermos (n)
toward (prep)
T-shirt, tee (n)

uh-huh (yes)
uh-uh (no)
universe (n)
upward (adv)

veranda (n)
voice mail (n)

wannabe (a, n)
website (n)
whiskey (n)
woolly (a)
wrought-iron (a)

x-ray (n)

young'un (n)

4

Characters

Characters are more than just names in the story. They each have a life of their own, in varying amounts of detail: their appearance, their personal history, their habits, and much more. And in the process of writing and revising, it's easy for inconsistencies in these "facts" to slip in. Keeping a detailed style sheet can help catch these errors, large or small. The copyeditor must also pay attention to whether characters are represented respectfully and authentically; see the section titled "Conscious language" in chapter 7.

Figures 4.1 and 4.2 at the end of the chapter illustrate two ways to format entries for the Characters section of your style sheet.

Organizing character lists

Every fiction style sheet should include a character list. A common format for character lists is just that: a tidy alphabetical list of character names, often last name first, first name last. We copyeditors love to make alphabetical lists, and such a list is wonderful for finding a name. But in order to ensure continuity in characters' attributes and relationships, let's see if we can improve on this format.

For example, suppose that in chapter 1, Ranjit is described as being a vegetarian, but in chapter 18 he orders a Big Mac. Or suppose that Althea is an only child in chapter 3, but in chapter 27 she gets a call from her sister. Human memory isn't always good enough to recall a detail from so far back—and such details are often mentioned in the barest passing, so they are easy to overlook. That's what the style sheet is for. Any detail that could possibly be contradicted later on goes on the style sheet. Examples showing how to do this follow shortly.

Back to organizing. So if we're not alphabetizing, what is a copyeditor to do?

GROUP BY AFFILIATION

I recommend grouping characters not alphabetically, but by their relationships to each other, to help you catch problems. Family members, coworker groups, the neighbors, the regulars down at the pub, the bad guys, the werewolves: these are examples of how you might group characters. Sometimes you may not be sure where to put a character. That's okay; start them in their own group for now, and later it may become clear. The groupings you choose depend on the content of the manuscript.[1] The advantage of grouping like this is that it helps you spot name changes (the maître d' was Antoine, but suddenly he's become Anatole), missing or extra people (there are supposed to be five Murphy brothers, but six are named), and so on. Some copyeditors divide characters into "major" and "minor" characters; however, this is another decision to make that doesn't add much information (and there are shades of "major" and "minor"), it doesn't change what sorts of things should be noted, and a minor character in one book is often a major character in a later one.[2]

"But how can anyone find the entry for a character if they're not alphabetical?" you might ask. When you're working electronically, you can simply run a quick search of your style sheet. You can also put all

1. As you review the sample style sheets in figures 4.1 and 4.2, don't worry if the groupings are not obvious to you. Remember that this is an internal production document for reference by those who are working with the manuscript (and have presumably read it). It will make sense in that context.

2. However, if I am working on a novel in a series and did not copyedit the previous books, and the character list on the previous style sheet is long and in alphabetical order, and particularly if the book is a fantasy with a complicated social hierarchy that would be difficult to tease out when you're coming in at the fourth book, I simply leave the character list as is, trusting that the relationships are well established, rather than try to reinvent the wheel. At this point, trying to reorganize the list would be unnecessary busywork. I still have the option of querying if something doesn't make sense.

main-entry character names in bold and use that in your search parameters to go directly to the right entry (see figures 4.1 and 4.2). And except for extremely long character lists (for series, cumulative character
lists can be twenty-five pages long!), often you might have to PgDn or
PgUp only a few screens to get to the entry you're looking for. You could
also add bookmarks in your style sheet for frequently accessed sections.

Some publishers and authors prefer a simple alphabetized list
(by first names or by last names, with or without annotations). You
can provide one by duplicating your annotated list and revising it as
requested—but send your original annotated list along too. It's part
of your work product, and your client may be pleasantly surprised by
how useful it is.

Figures 4.1 and 4.2 illustrate two possible ways to format your annotated character list. Figure 4.1 shows the way I have been doing it for
years: factual entries grouped together on separate lines, for example,
physical appearance, then personal history, and other items as appropriate, with the relevant chapter number(s) in the right margin. This
method allows for more complex groupings—say, detailed descriptions of particular life events, with sublist entries indented under the
main entry "Miguel Torres." This type of list is easy to visually skim and
organize. Figure 4.2 consolidates all factual entries for a character in
a single run-in list, with relevant chapter numbers after each entry in
parentheses. This method takes up less space and works well with less
complex lists, or if you have received a character list in a similar format and will simply be adding to it. This type of list also makes it very
easy to sort the entries and provide an alphabetized list, if requested.

ADD HEADINGS

Insert headings as needed (Neela's Family, Vampires, Townspeople,
Squadron Seven) and/or graphics such as horizontal rules to identify
and divide your groupings. Organize entries within the group to help
you see relationships. For example, you might list a main character;
then her closest sister, who's a secondary protagonist; then her other
siblings and their spouses and children; and then their parents. List
them by the name they're primarily known as, followed by any formal
titles, ranks, nicknames, or aliases as they turn up during the edit.
This makes variations among multiple names easy to spot.

LABEL QUERIED ITEMS

As described at the beginning of chapter 3, identify any entries that you queried in the manuscript, to alert future reviewers of the manuscript and style sheet that the query needs to be resolved:

(?) = queried in ms. (at the top of the style sheet)
blond (or brown)(?) hair (in the character entry)

What counts as a character?

Your character list may contain more than just fictional human beings who have names. Here are some examples and things to watch out for.

ANIMALS

Animals are characters too. You might identify animals separately in some way. I enclose animal names in quotes on the style sheet; some other editors put them in a separate list. Add unnamed animals too; make sure that the neighbors' black Lab doesn't turn into a border collie.

"Josie": liver-and-white springer spaniel; 8 years old; born in
February

IMPORTANT OBJECTS, SENTIENT OBJECTS, DEITIES

Especially in fantasy and science fiction, you may encounter "characters" that are important or sentient objects such as weapons and other magical items (think of the elven blade Sting from Tolkien's *Lord of the Rings* or the Sorting Hat in the Harry Potter books), as well as fictional deities, spirits, and so forth. On the style sheet they go, along with their characteristics and abilities.

UNNAMED CHARACTERS

Just because a character has no name doesn't mean that their details won't be treated inconsistently, or that they won't show up later (just as with animals). Record them on your character list too.

bartender: graying hair, mustache

REAL PEOPLE

Real people who appear as characters require slightly different treatment from fictional ones. Fact-check names, dates, and other attributes: Were they alive during the timeline of the story, and is their age correct? Were they famous in the story at the same time that they were famous in reality? Are they fictionalized for story purposes? (Writers of historical fiction often do this and explain in an afterword. Check for any such notes before querying.) See also the section titled "Real people and other entities" in chapter 9 for a discussion of the potential pitfalls of mentioning real people in a fictional work.

Track more than just names of people

What kinds of details should you track? Anything that could possibly be contradicted later. (And as you come across such items later, check against your previous entries on the style sheet to ensure that they are still accurate; if not, you know that you need to flag or query.) For example, suppose Beck is described as "tall" in chapter 2. If he's six foot three in chapter 8, that checks out against chapter 2, and you can add his exact height to the style sheet. But if in chapter 19 he's shorter than someone who's been described as being "average height," there's a problem and you'll need to query.

Here are some suggestions for adding information to your character list:

- Copy descriptive phrases from the manuscript into the style sheet, for ease of searching later if you need to refer to earlier text. You can condense the copied text by changing spelled-out numbers to digits and editing down to essential key words. For example, *her auburn hair cascaded down her back, and fluffy bangs accentuated her ocean-blue eyes* (in the manuscript) would become auburn hair down her back, bangs, blue eyes (on the style sheet); *died six days before his eighty-fifth birthday* would become died 6 days before his 85th birthday. You can take out information that's nonessential to the style sheet (you might copy a full paragraph just to grab a few informational phrases).

- Note that descriptive entries in your Characters section don't need to conform to the editorial style for the manuscript. This is an internal document, so you can abbreviate things like *six feet, six inches tall* (in the manuscript) to 6′6″ tall (on the character list), omit articles (*a, an, the*), or use US spelling even if the style for the manuscript is UK spelling. Just make sure that proper names and story facts are correct.
- Don't make assumptions about the meaning of information from the manuscript. For example, just because Rhonda attended UCLA does not mean that she earned a degree there; Whitney Hutchins's husband may be introduced as "Tony," but his surname is not necessarily also Hutchins. Record the information exactly as stated, without extrapolating.
- Pay attention to absolute words that are used to describe characters and their habits: *never, always, only, favorite*, and the like. Record descriptions like has never smoked and only wears boxers; they are clues to potential contradictions later on.
- Under each character's entry, group similar types of description together, even when they come from different places in the manuscript, for ease of reference. For example, you might list physical descriptions first, then personal history, then significant objects (jewelry the person always wears, descriptions of vehicles they own, etc.), and so on.
- Relative descriptions are important too:

  Rodrigo towers over Lancelot
  Elodie is 2 years older than Sean

- On your style sheet, use chapter numbers (if provided) rather than page numbers to identify where information appears; the manuscript's page numbers are likely to change during production, but chapter numbers probably won't. (See the section titled "Receiving the manuscript" in chapter 2.) You can always search for the exact text (such as blue eyes); the chapter number helps narrow your search if you're having difficulty finding what you're looking for and need to visually skim the text instead.

The following are some examples of character attributes that you should record.

PHYSICAL DESCRIPTIONS

Physical descriptions of characters may include the following: hair color/length/qualities, eye/skin color, glasses/contacts, facial descriptions (*straight nose, thick eyebrows, high cheekbones*), height and build (*tall* or *five foot six, muscle-bound* or *lanky*), scars and tattoos, location of injuries, right/left distinctions, handedness, blood type, clothing size, disabilities, and vocal quality (pitch, accent).

blue eyes, pointed ears, 6 feet tall
shot in left thigh; missing his right eye

- Appearances can change: hair grows or is cut, children grow into adults, people gain and lose weight. Watch the passage of time on your timeline (see chapter 6) to be sure that the time frame is appropriate (if Daryl was bald two months ago, how is he now running his hands through his lush wavy hair?) and that major changes in appearance are explained, either directly or by inference (the formerly plump barmaid is now gaunt after a year of famine); if not, query.
- In fantasy and science fiction, characters often change appearance by magical means: Anya's eyes are blue in human form but golden in wolf form. Rolf's tattoos glow when he is angry. Record these conditional appearance aspects as well as those that don't change, and double-check them when they appear.
- Watch for "food" descriptions of appearance, especially for people of color (*mocha skin, caramel eyes*). These terms can be dehumanizing and objectifying (people are not food), often refer to commodities produced by enslaved people (coffee, chocolate), and are cliché at best and racist at worst. The same is true for words like *exotic* that treat people as "other," as well as stereotypical colors that have been used to describe skin tone (such as *red* or *copper* for Native people or *yellow* for Asians). Always query such usage; explain why it might offend some readers and suggest finding a different way to

describe the character (if it's even necessary at all). The fact that a person is not white can be conveyed or suggested in more appropriate ways (*his deep brown complexion*; *my braids swung as I shook my head*). And check to see whether the author includes just as much description for white people; characters should not be assumed to be white unless they are specifically described as not white. (White people have skin tones too: pale, ruddy, golden, tanned, freckled . . .).

Also beware of stereotypical descriptions of characters' behavior, such as Native people wearing beads and speaking in one-word sentences, Black people being loud and mouthy, Asians being mysterious, lesbians wearing boots and flannel, and so on. Readers, particularly those who share an identity with such characters, are likely not to appreciate the broad and potentially offensive brush.

Note: If you are working for a publisher, contact your project manager to discuss these concerns. Your goal is not only to be a stand-in for the reader but also to respect the author's representation of their culture, especially when it is different from your own. For example, an Asian author has probably portrayed their Asian characters exactly as they would like to. Proceed with caution if your experience does not provide you with the appropriate background to question those choices. (See also the section titled "Conscious language" in chapter 7 for further discussion.)

PERSONAL STORY

A character's personal story includes the following: gender identity and pronouns, age/birthday, sexual orientation, relationships, education (including current grade in school or year in college), past and present employment, abilities, nicknames, habits, vehicles they own or drive, favorite things, accents, pet phrases, and major life events.

age 27; her birthday was last May; the baby will be born next fall
just turned 24; her brother is 2 years older
age 9; in 4th grade
her mother died of cancer when she was 12

he has been divorced twice
PhD from Harvard; they have been a CPA for 8 years
she has a brother and a sister
vegetarian; doesn't drink
attends group therapy on Tuesday mornings
telepath; spent 3 years in Paris
he becomes female in panther form
avid golfer; favorite drink is rum and Coke
inherited $6 million from his grandmother

- When a story runs several years or decades, characters' ages obviously change. Track these as well, referring to your timeline (see chapter 6) to keep them accurate.
- Record relative ages as well as exact numbers and dates, if they are given. Double-check that Xue's brother, two years older than she is, doesn't age faster and become ten years older—or younger! If Molly turns twenty-four in the springtime (in the Northern Hemisphere), make sure she doesn't have a birthday in November. If Philomena was a baby in 1938 and is now an octogenarian, and she helped her grandson open a business ten years ago in 2004 (which would make her seventy-six), something is wrong. Query time! Double-check all those tiny details to make sure they hang together.
- Characters each have their own pronouns (*he, she, they . . .*). Gender-neutral pronouns may be *they/them/their, e/em/eir*, or some other form. Some characters may use more than one set of pronouns (*she/they*). Include pronouns next to each character's name for easy reference, as well as using those pronouns in their character description. (See figures 4.1 and 4.2 for examples.) Do not assume a character's gender until it is stated. I once copyedited a novel in which a character's gender was deliberately not revealed until late in the story—and it was very cleverly done. (Including everyone's pronouns not only promotes an inclusive mindset but also makes it obvious when a character's gender is not stated.) Also note that a character's gender may be fluid and change as the story progresses; query

'the author if you are unsure whether this is deliberate. See also the section titled "Conscious language" in chapter 7.

- Details are especially important in series fiction, where facts sometimes change or get lost across books. If Phillip worked his way through college as a lifeguard in book 2, he should not be afraid to dive into a lake to save someone in book 5 without a good reason.
- Pay attention to what these details mean for the plot. For example, if a person is a vegetarian, they might order a cheese omelet but probably not a cheeseburger. (And certainly not the veal piccata!)

PHONE NUMBERS, EMAIL AND POSTAL ADDRESSES, SOCIAL MEDIA USERNAMES

The trappings of modern life apply to fictional characters just as they do to people in the real world: phone numbers, street addresses, email addresses, and usernames for Facebook, Twitter, Instagram, Reddit, and numerous other online forums. What other numbers and ID do characters have? Vehicle license plate numbers, bank account numbers, student ID numbers, sports uniform numbers? Record them all.

If characters' phone numbers, email addresses, usernames, and other types of contact information are mentioned, they should be either completely fictional (such as *foxy13@talkplace.com*, where *talkplace.com* is an inactive domain, or a *555-####* phone number); "out of service" because the author has reserved the username; or incomplete so they are unusable. (See also the section titled "Deliberate obfuscation and fictionalization" in chapter 9.) Query the author if these elements appear to be real and usable.

NEGATIVE ATTRIBUTES

It's just as important to record mentions of things that a character can't do, has never done, refuses to do, doesn't own, doesn't like, and so on as it is to track things they can, will, have, and do. Pay attention to absolute words like *never*, *always*, and *only* when used to describe a character. Such statements can be prime setups for plot holes later.

> can't swim, hates cigarette smoke
> afraid of dogs, has never left the country

CHARACTERS WHO ARE DEAD OR DIE DURING THE COURSE OF THE STORY

Resurrections (and they do happen in fiction!) should be intentional, not accidental. Identify characters who are dead when the story begins, as well as those who die during the course of the story, whether "onstage" or offstage. How and where did they die? Did the death occur in real time in the story, or was it reported later by someone who was there? If it was not a natural death, who or what killed them? Did anyone witness their death? What happened to their remains? These notes can be useful in later chapters of a long novel or for later books in a series.

> killed by Diego (stabbed in the abdomen)
> died of a heart attack when Chantelle was 14; she found him

CONFUSABLE CHARACTER NAMES

Names are names, and anyone can have a particular name, and people have similar names in real life. However, names in fiction that are too similar can make things confusing. If the reader has to stop to remember the difference between Sheila, Sylvia, and Shauna, that's a distraction that pulls them out of the story. Or maybe Viktor was a minor character mentioned twice in chapter 3, and here's a Viktor in a completely different situation in chapter 29; is it the same person or a remarkable coincidence? If you notice that a third of the characters have names that start with *K*, it's time to query the author and ask them to consider changing a few for variety and to avoid confusion.

Fixing these issues is easier if only one major character is involved; if chapter 29 Viktor is important but chapter 3 Viktor is merely background, query the author to change the name in chapter 3. If more characters are involved, ask the author to review all of the names to decide which ones to change.

Also watch for character names that are similar or identical to that of a real, well-known person, unless there's a reason for it (for example, they were named after someone, or the plot requires that they be confused with that person). Readers may be distracted by a character who happens to be named "Tony Morrison" for no apparent reason, because they will pause and think of the similarly named author. Using a real person's name can also be problematic if the character has negative attributes that the real person may not want associated with their name. Flag the passage with a query to the author or publisher. (See also the section titled "Real people and other entities" in chapter 9.)

Finally, pay attention to characters with initials as names. Is it *AJ*, *A.J.*, or *A. J.*? (The first two are the most common choices when used as a stand-alone name.) Run a separate search to catch discrepancies.

What if you find a contradiction?

Oops. Judith is blond in chapter 4 but brunette in chapter 27. Orlando's eyes keep changing color from brown to green to brown again. Tonya's parents died when she was a baby, but they also threw her out of the house when she was sixteen. What to do?

- If it's a minor detail that's not critical to the plot, and only a few instances are different (suppose Judith's hair is described as blond twelve times and brown twice), it's safe to simply change the brown hair back to blond and write a query at the first instance alerting the author to the change.
- If Orlando's eyes are brown six times and green seven times, it's better to query and let the author choose a color. Highlight or query each instance to help the author catch them all.
- Let's say that the fact that Tonya is an orphan is important to the plot, but so is the fact that she was thrown out of her home and had to fend for herself at a young age. That's not something that a copyeditor can fix; the author is in charge of plot adjustment or rewriting. But when you query the author about the discrepancy, you can suggest a possible solution: maybe after her parents' deaths, Tonya was raised by an aunt and uncle, and they could be the ones who threw her out. Be clear that this is only a suggestion; the author may let it go, or they may be grateful for a solution that might not have occurred to them, or they may solve it another way.

- You may find a plot hole that has no obvious solution. For example, suppose Luna grew up with her brother Saul in the previous book in the series, but this book states that she grew up as an only child. The best you can do then is outline the problem and ask the author if they can see a way to solve it. After that, it's in the author's hands—and the author may decide to just live with it. But you've done your due diligence.

Note: PB denotes information from *Previous Book.*
(?) = queried in ms.

Miguel Torres (he)	**(Ch. #)**
dark brown eyes; blond hair; tall; tattoo on his left biceps (wolf and crescent moon)	1, 8
his great-grandfather **Juan Torres** traveled to WY and started the ranch	1
worked in Boise until his father died, about 6 years ago	2
his mother abandoned him as an infant	22
his girlfriend **Tia** dumped him 10 years ago; single ever since	22
drives a camo-painted Ford F-150	31
"Wink"—brown mutt; male; one eye; Miguel found him as a stray puppy	1

Louis (?) Reed (he)	
age 42; tall (6′6″); about 180 pounds; brown hair	22, 28
lost his right arm below the elbow in a construction accident when he was 20	24
grew up in Phoenix; has 2 younger brothers	32
drives a beat-up 4×4 truck	26, 34
Terrence Reed (he)—Louis's father; owns a hardware store in Phoenix	32

Karen Elizabeth Hayes (she)	
age 25; blue eyes; wavy blond hair; 5′1″; curvy	PB, 2, 17
grew up in Ohio; left as soon as she graduated from high school	PB
attended college for a year	PB
parents were killed in a car accident when she was a baby; raised by a surly aunt	PB, 6
Johnny calls her **"Kitty"**	PB
broken collarbone (left); bruised on the left side of her face	19

Eunice Russell (she)	
lives in a tiny house just off the town square	PB
never married, no children; her parents are buried in the family plot on the farm	PB
was a nurse for 47 years; now she volunteers at the hospital	PB
"Sparky"—Eunice's cat; female, black, green eyes	PB

Eldon Russell (he)	
Eunice's cousin; age 92; lived in Pleasantville his whole life	PB, 3, 17
unkempt silver hair and beard; leathery face; short and stocky	PB
drives a dirty blue truck; also has a golf cart; worked as a blacksmith	PB
was estranged from Eunice until 5 years ago	PB

Figure 4.1. Sample style sheet: characters (descriptive entries on separate lines)

Sam (Samantha) Woodson (she)
age 31; moved back to Pleasantville 5 years ago; has a degree in history   PB
tall, brunette; hazel eyes   PB
had just graduated when Frank died; elected mayor the following year (4 years ago)   PB

Frank Woodson (he)
Sam's father (she refers to him as "Frank")   PB
former mayor; died 5 years ago; stabbed in the chest in an alley   PB, 18
his killer was found 6 months later and was later killed in prison   18

James Woodson (he)
age 25; Sam's brother; was little when they moved off the ranch   4, 20
his best friend in high school was **Rocky**   4
tall, lanky; sandy hair, hazel eyes   PB, 26

Sheriff Luke Farrell (he)—one of Sam's suitors   PB
Christopher George (he)—was mayor before Frank Woodson   38

Hunter Ford (he)
blond hair; blue eyes; about 36 (5 years older than Sam)   PB, 4
drives a green Chevy Tahoe   PB, 24
on the town council; has worked at the hotel since high school   PB
visits Eunice every Wednesday afternoon   8

Jennie (she)—Hunter's adopted daughter; age 11; red hair; calls Hunter **"Papa"**   PB
"Sable"—Jennie's black miniature poodle; female   25

Maggie Ford (she)
Hunter's sister; age 25   PB
long blond hair; tall; blue eyes; birthday is August 12   4, 9, 24, 31
drives a black Honda Civic   PB
went to culinary school; had one previous job   PB, 3
her husband **Roberto** was killed by a drunk driver a month after their wedding   4, 14

Janet Ford (she)
Hunter's mother; in her late 50s; runs the hotel in town and does catering   PB
drives a blue panel van   PB
hosts book club on the 1st Tuesday of the month   14, 26

Quinn (they)
Hunter's cousin; 26; short, curvy; blue eyes; short, curly blond hair   PB, 29
recently moved back to Pleasantville after a messy breakup   4, 31
drives a silver Prius   29

RANCH HANDS

Johnny Sleeping Bear (he)
grew up in an orphanage; moved to Pleasantville 2 years ago   PB
short and thin; dark hair in a buzz cut; youngest of the ranch hands   PB
does charcoal drawings; his favorite dessert is peach cobbler   28

Tom Knight (he)—tall; shaggy blond hair; star quarterback in high school   PB
Hector Morales (he)—tall, broad shoulders; dark hair, dark eyes; was in the army   PB

Louise (?) Simpson (she)
teller at the bank; thin; middle-aged; waitressed at the diner in high school   3
had a baby when she was a teenager; gave it up for adoption   38

Genie Simpson (she)
mid-50s; slightly overweight; same height as Louise   4, 23, 39
had a heart attack last year; had a triple bypass   38
has been working at the garage for 23 years   38

Clayton Blackwolf (he)
farrier; in his 50s; tall and stout   PB, 6
his family moved to Pleasantville when he was a teen   PB
     youngest of 7 kids; 3 older brothers, then 3 older sisters, then Clayton   PB
drives a rusty Buick; uses a flip phone   PB, 6, 28

Jane McKenzie (she)
late 30s; ash-blond hair, green eyes; slender; tall (5′ 8″) and curvy   PB, 28
her father was an alcoholic   PB

Mitchell Stone (he)
age 19; short and stocky; dark hair   7
his father is an accountant; mother teaches English at the high school   12
drives a beat-up Chevy pickup   23, 37

Isabel Garza (she)—town gossip; middle aged, chain smoker   PB, 21
Kelly (she/they)—server at the diner; age 16; spiky black hair   5, 8

CHARACTERS FROM PREVIOUS BOOKS (not mentioned)

Silvia Hernandez (she)—librarian
Lindsey (she)—red hair
Winona Rhodes (she)—town clerk; middle-aged; wire-rimmed glasses
Bill Rhodes (she)—Winona's husband
Thomas Berry (he)—jeweler

CHARACTERS
Fabulous Author, *Contemporary Series Romance*

Note: (##) = chapter number; PB denotes information from *Previous Book.*
(?) = queried in ms.

Miguel Torres (he): dark brown eyes, blond hair (PB); tall (1); tattoo on his left biceps (wolf
and crescent moon) (8); his great-grandfather **Juan Torres** traveled to WY and started
the ranch (1); worked in Boise until his father died, about 6 years ago (2); his mother
abandoned him as an infant (22); his girlfriend **Tia** dumped him 10 years ago; single ever
since (22); drives a camo-painted Ford F-150 (31)
"Wink"—brown mutt; male; one eye; Miguel found him as a stray puppy (1)

Louis (?) Reed (he): age 42, tall (6′6″), about 180 pounds (22); brown hair (28); lost his right
arm below the elbow in a construction accident when he was 20 (24); grew up in
Phoenix, has 2 younger brothers (32); drives a beat-up 4×4 truck (26, 32)
Terrence Reed (he): Louis's father; owns a hardware store in Phoenix (32)

Karen Elizabeth Hayes (she): age 25, blue eyes, wavy blond hair (PB); 5′1″, curvy (17); grew
up in Ohio, left as soon as she graduated from high school, attended college for a year
(PB); parents were killed in a car accident when she was a baby (PB); raised by a surly
aunt (6); Johnny calls her **"Kitty"** (PB); broken collarbone (left), bruised on the left side
of her face (19)
Eunice Russell (she): lives in a tiny house just off the town square, never married, no children,
her parents are buried in the family plot on the farm; was a nurse for 47 years, now she
volunteers at the hospital (PB)
"Sparky"—Eunice's cat; female, black, green eyes (PB)
Eldon Russell (he): Eunice's cousin (PB); age 92 (3); lived in Pleasantville his whole life (17);
unkempt silver hair and beard; leathery face; short and stocky;;drives a dirty blue truck;
also has a golf cart; worked as a blacksmith;was estranged from Eunice until 5 years ago
(PB)

Sam (Samantha) Woodson (she): age 31; moved back to Pleasantville 5 years ago; has a degree
in history; tall, brunette; hazel eyes; had just graduated when Frank died; elected mayor
the following year (4 years ago) (PB)
Frank Woodson (he): Sam's father (she refers to him as "Frank"), former mayor (PB); died 5
years ago, stabbed in the chest in an alley (18); his killer was found 6 months later and
was later killed in prison (18)
James Woodson (he): age 25, Sam's brother (25); was little when they moved off the ranch
(20); his best friend in high school was **Rocky** (4); tall, lanky (PB); sandy hair, hazel eyes
(26)

Sheriff Luke Farrell (he): one of Sam's suitors (PB)
Christopher George (he): was mayor before Frank Woodson (38)

Figure 4.2. Sample style sheet: characters (descriptive entries run-in)

Hunter Ford (he): blond hair, blue eyes (PB); about 36 (5 years older than Sam) (4); drives a green (PB) Chevy Tahoe (24); on the town council, has worked at the hotel since high school (PB); visits Eunice every Wednesday afternoon (8)

Jennie (she): Hunter's adopted daughter; age 11; red hair; calls Hunter **"Papa"** (PB)

"Sable"—Jennie's black miniature poodle; female (25)

Maggie Ford (she): Hunter's sister, age 25 (PB); long blond hair, tall, blue eyes (4, 9, 24); birthday is August 12 (31); drives a black Honda Civic (PB); went to culinary school (PB); had one previous job (3); her husband **Roberto** was killed by a drunk driver a month after their wedding (4, 14)

Janet Ford (she): Hunter's mother, in her late 50s, runs the hotel in town and does catering, drives a blue panel van (PB); hosts book club on the 1st Tuesday of the month (14, 26)

Quinn (they): Hunter's cousin, age 26, short, curvy, blue eyes; short, curly blond hair (PB, 29); recently moved back to P'ville after a messy breakup (4, 31); drives a silver Prius (29)

RANCH HANDS

Johnny Sleeping Bear (he): grew up in an orphanage; moved to Pleasantville 2 years ago; short and thin; dark hair in a buzz cut; youngest of the ranch hands (PB); does charcoal drawings, his favorite dessert is peach cobbler (28)

Tom Knight (he): tall; shaggy blond hair; star quarterback in high school (PB)

Hector Morales (he): tall, broad shoulders; dark hair, dark eyes; was in the army (PB)

Louise (?) Simpson (she): teller at the bank, thin, middle-aged, waitressed at the diner in high school (3); had a baby when she was a teenager; gave it up for adoption (38)

Genie Simpson (she): mid-50s (4); slightly overweight(23); same height as Louise (39); had a heart attack last year, had a triple bypass, has worked at the garage for 23 years (38)

Clayton Blackwolf (he): farrier, in his 50s, tall and stout (PB, 6); his family moved to Pleasantville when he was a teen, youngest of 7 kids, 3 older brothers, then 3 older sisters, then Clayton (PB); drives a rusty Buick (PB, 6); uses a flip phone (28)

Jane McKenzie (she): late 30s, ash-blond hair, green eyes (PB); slender; tall (5′ 8″) and curvy (28); her father was an alcoholic (PB)

Mitchell Stone (he): age 19, short and stocky, dark hair (7); his father is an accountant, mother teaches English at the high school (12); drives a beat-up Chevy pickup (23, 37)

Isabel Garza (she): town gossip, middle aged, chain smoker (PB, 21)

Kelly (she/they): server at the diner, age 16, spiky black hair (5, 8)

CHARACTERS FROM PREVIOUS BOOKS (not mentioned)

Silvia Hernandez (she): librarian

Lindsey (she): red hair

Winona Rhodes (she): town clerk; middle-aged; wire-rimmed glasses

Bill Rhodes (she): Winona's husband

Thomas Berry (he): jeweler

5

Places

In a work of fiction, the characters move around the world they inhabit: within buildings and throughout neighborhoods, cities, and even sometimes spiritual realms. Let's talk about how to keep that motion logical. Many of the concepts discussed in chapter 4 apply here as well.

In chapter 4 I talked about the practice of listing characters alphabetically, and how doing so isn't helpful for maintaining continuity. And so it is with geographical details. Grouping places by their relation to each other—a country (or planet) and all the cities in (or on) it, a house with all its interior and exterior details, shops that are near each other, streets and how they are connected—will make continuity problems stand out. The groupings you choose will depend on the content of the manuscript.

One exception to the no-alphabetizing concept is that after the edit is done, you may have a list of minor features such as streets, rivers, or businesses that do not have extra information associated with them. These can be alphabetized by category—all the streets, all the rivers, and so on—just for ease of finding them.

Many novels are set in real locations, and you'll need to check whether the details reflect reality. Have you ever read a novel set in a location you know well and scoffed when a street ran in the wrong direction or a building was miles away from its real location? When specifics are given, check them out. Get out your atlas or pull up an online map. However, remember that authors often introduce deliberate fictionalization, just as phone numbers in movies and on television are often of the "555" variety. So when you find such discrepancies, query them and ask whether they are deliberate. (See also the section titled "Deliberate obfuscation and fictionalization" in chapter 9.)

For fictional locations such as towns, planets, or fantasy worlds, consider drawing a map to help you (and the characters) keep your bearings. This prevents you from having the town hall and tavern next door to each other in chapter 5 and across the street from each other in chapter 17.

Figures 5.1 and 5.2 at the end of the chapter illustrate two ways to format entries for the Places section of your style sheet, similar to the methods described in chapter 4 for figures 4.1 and 4.2.

Details to track

The suggestions from chapter 4 for deciding what character attributes to track also apply for places. Let's review them here and add a few more.

- Record details that could be contradicted later. If Irina's bedroom window faces west, we don't want her awakened in the morning by the blinding sun. Don't let a solid wooden door turn into steel. And so on. (And as you come across such items later, check them against existing style sheet entries to ensure that they are still accurate; if not, you'll need to flag or query.)
- Copy descriptive phrases from the manuscript into the style sheet, for ease of searching later if you need to refer to earlier text. You can condense the copied text by changing spelled-out numbers to digits and editing down to essential key words. For example, *Zoe found a posh flat on Camden Street that shortened her commute to a fifteen-minute walk* (in the manuscript) would become Zoe's flat: posh, on Camden St; 15-min. walk to work (on the style sheet); *The Brau Haus with its heavy oak doors was the jewel of downtown; it had been in business for more than a hundred years* would become the Brau Haus: downtown; heavy oak doors; in business over 100 years (on the style sheet). You can take out information

that's nonessential to the style sheet (you might copy a full paragraph just to grab a few informational phrases).

- Note that descriptive entries for your Places section don't need to conform to the editorial style for the manuscript. This is an internal document, so you can abbreviate things like *seventy-five miles* or *north-northwest* (in the manuscript) to 75 miles or NNW (in the Places section), omit articles (*a, an, the*), or use US spelling even if the style for the manuscript is UK spelling. Just make sure that proper names and story facts are correct.

- Don't make assumptions about the meaning of information from the manuscript. For example, two streets can intersect, but also both run mainly north and south; the bakery can be on the corner but also across the street. Record the information exactly as stated, without extrapolating.

- How much detail do you need to record about every place that characters visit? Let your first reading pass through the manuscript be your guide. It will tell you the overall level of detail (are houses just houses, or are there descriptions of their architecture, landscaping, color scheme, interiors, and so on?) and which places make frequent appearances (and thus are more likely candidates for discrepancies throughout the story). If a location's details are mentioned frequently, record them and check the style sheet each time they're mentioned. If you're not sure whether you'll need to refer back to a detailed description in the manuscript, you can add a note such as Detailed description in Ch. 2 to the style sheet, so you know where to go if you need to check something.

- Group similar types of description together, even when they come from different places in the manuscript, for ease of reference. For example, you might describe the exterior of a house, then the entryway and ground floor, then upper floors, and so on.

- Relative descriptions are important too. If the office complex towers over the hotel, then someone on the top floor of the hotel can't look down on the office building's roof. If Henry's friend Zack lives close by, but Simon lives across town, then Zack and Simon can't live next door to each other.

- Use chapter numbers (if provided) rather than page numbers on your style sheet to identify where information appears; page numbers are likely to change during production, but chapter numbers probably won't. (See the section titled "Receiving the manuscript" in chapter 2.) You can always search for the exact text (such as picket fence); the chapter number helps narrow your search if you're having difficulty finding what you're looking for and need to visually skim the text instead.
- As described at the beginning of chapter 3, identify any entries that you queried in the manuscript, to alert future reviewers of the manuscript and style sheet that the query needs to be resolved:

(?) = queried in ms. (at the top of the style sheet)
Harry's office is on the 2nd/3rd (?) floor (in the Places section)

The following are some examples of place attributes that you should record.

General information

Descriptions of places may mention any of the following: names, history, cardinal directions, distances, right/left distinctions, business hours and events, and descriptions of exteriors and interiors. We'll look at each of these in more detail.

NAMES

Named locations may include planets, countries, regions, cities and towns, streets, geographical features, businesses, and buildings. Record the capping and spelling of proper nouns (including real names that might be spelled different ways: *Walmart, 7-Eleven*), and fact-check real locations. It's helpful to group locations geographically: each city as a main head, with all the locations, streets, and so on within it underneath.

Just as for character names (see chapter 4), query fictional business names that are similar or identical to a real one. (See the section titled "Real people and other entities" in chapter 9 for discussion of how this can cause problems.)

the Waldorf Building, the village of Snodsbury
the Bluebell Diner (aka Blue's)
the War Room
Hyperion VII (planet; not 7)

HISTORY

Both real and fictional locations may have a history. The town was founded in 1861; planet Yargan was terraformed for human habitation near the end of the Third Era; the deli was built on the site of the Chinese restaurant that burned down two years ago. Record these facts in case they're needed for cross-checking later. Check that the history of real locations aligns with the timeline of the story.

CARDINAL DIRECTIONS AND DISTANCES

Cardinal directions and distances are important whether real or fictional. Fact-check real ones, and make sure that fictional ones make sense. Consider the fictional town of Midvale in the following examples; if Midvale is in Illinois, a three-hour drive to St. Louis is possible. If Midvale is in Arizona, that's a problem that needs a query. Similarly, if Benny can walk to the comedy club from his apartment (a few miles) in the time it takes to smoke a cigarette, something is off.

the mountains are west of town
Midvale is a 3-hour drive from St. Louis
the comedy club is a few miles from Benny's apartment
the laundromat is at the southwest corner of the intersection

- Note how this point also relates to the timeline, discussed in chapter 6: if the characters take a day to travel from point A to point B, but a week to return, either there's a problem with the number of days that have passed during that return trip, or there should be a good reason for the delay.
- Also watch the relationships between locations: If a hotel is just outside the city limits, how can the bar across the street from the hotel be five miles out? What can (and can't) a person see when looking out the front windows of the realty office? (Hint: Not the customer inside the pet store a block down the

street.) This is where grouping by location can help you catch inconsistencies.

- Record concrete directions (north, south, and so on) as well as things that indicate or suggest directions, such as sun and moon positions and orientations of coastlines and borders.

> the morning sun streamed through the window
> the main road is 5 miles south of the border

RIGHT/LEFT DISTINCTIONS

When you get to the end of the block, do you turn right or left to get to the embassy? Are the wizard's rooms in the right or left wing of the palace? Record the information and make sure it's the same throughout. This applies to both interior and exterior locations, and we'll see more examples later.

> there's a bathroom on the right
> Violet's house is past the brewery, left on King Street, and then
>   right onto Sullivan Square

BUSINESS HOURS AND REGULAR EVENTS

Record times and days of regular events associated with a location; then when you record those events on your timeline (see chapter 6), you can cross-check that they're happening on the right day. (If the book club always meets at Beans & Books on Thursdays, then what are they doing there on a Saturday?)

This is also a good place to record other business details:

> the gift shop is closed on Mondays
> the soccer team practices every Wednesday at 6 pm
> the diner is famous for its Hokey Pokey Pie; has a catfish special
>   on Thursdays

Exteriors

Descriptions of exteriors include geography, distances, navigation, architecture, landscaping, and various other aspects of the outside world. Record details and picture the scene: does it make sense?

(There's no such thing as a three-story bungalow.) Let's consider some of these elements in more detail.

GEOGRAPHY

Geography implies places on Earth, real or fictional, such as countries, cities, mountains, rivers, roads, public transportation, buildings, large military vessels such as battleships, and other features; in fantasy and sci-fi, it may include magical realms, planets and galaxies, and associated features such as suns and moons, political divisions, spaceships, habitats, and whatever physical (and metaphysical) locations the author might invent. Look up real places and see if they make sense. Check the map: Does that street run in that direction? Does that subway route work? Does that mountain range cross that border? Does that river flow north or south? For fictional elements, you're creating your own reference, so be as detailed as possible. Draw a map if it helps you (and be prepared to revise it if it turns out that you misinterpreted something). Sometimes the author includes informative front or back matter describing the fictional world, its magic, and so on, and maybe even a map. Use these as your primary references; add them to the style sheet and build on them, adding new information from the manuscript as you edit.

> the mountains to the south
> the Phoenix system (twin suns)
> Evermore: ethereal plane; accessible only through the portal in
>   Fintan Wood

DISTANCES

Distances matter, and they are often interrelated with time (see the section titled "Time Zones and Travel Times" in chapter 6). For real locations, Google Maps can help you check distances and travel times. For stories set in locations that aren't on current maps, let the story be your guide. Record details and refer to maps that you've drawn or the author has provided.

> a 10-minute drive to the station
> Featherstonehaugh Castle: 10 days' travel on horseback from
>   the Heath

Alice's hotel room has a view of the London Eye
Scorpio B (planet): 25 light-years from the center of the galaxy

NAVIGATION

Characters don't usually stay in one place; they move around their
world, and their movements should make sense. Check real maps
such as Google Maps for real locations and directions, and refer to
fictional maps that you've created or been given. Pay attention to
right and left turns as they relate to cardinal directions. Distances are
also interrelated to navigation and time; put yourself in the scene and
see if the route seems possible. (This works for interiors as well as exteriors; two people will probably not have a five-minute conversation
while riding an elevator up three floors.)

ARCHITECTURE

Buildings and other places have elements that can be overlooked in
revisions and lead to discrepancies: architectural style, size of lot,
type and shape of roof, number and type of windows and doors, color
and type of siding and trim, porches, balconies, gables, staircases,
and so on. Recording these details helps you catch the two-car garage
that turns into a three-car garage twelve chapters later. Look up real
places and see if the description matches. Pay attention to the words
floor and *ground* (what people stand on); floors are inside and the
ground is outside. (*You take the couch, and I'll sleep on the ground*
needs a word change if the setting is a living room.)

2-story house; built in the 1940s
wraparound porch with 3 steps
neat flower boxes at every window
Dani's rented flat is on the 4th floor, next to the staircase, back
     of the building

LANDSCAPING

Pay attention to landscaping and other outdoor elements: trees and
plantings, gazebos, trellises, fences, outdoor lighting, driveways and
walkways, pools, sheds, and so on. Can those plants grow in that
location? Is the driveway gravel or paved, curved or straight? Does

the low stone fence in chapter 3 become a white picket fence in chapter 19?

> 5 large oak trees
> a flagstone path from the small front porch to the sidewalk
> the cemetery is not fenced
> the rear deck overlooks the pool and the woods beyond

Interiors

Descriptions of interiors include the layout of rooms, windows, doors, hallways, and staircases; décor and construction; right/left distinctions; and number of stories. They also cover cardinal and other directions (the windows face the setting sun; the balcony looks out over the ocean). Record these descriptions and picture the scene: Does it make sense? (That door was solid wood yesterday, so how can she be looking through it into the street when it's closed and locked? And does it swing in or out?) Check later descriptions against previous ones for consistency.

LAYOUT

Every interior has a structural layout, and unless there is a reason for it to change (remodeling, arson, magical transformation, act of God), it should remain consistent throughout. What floor is each room on? Are they large or small? Where is the kitchen, bathroom, family room, office?

> foyer leads to a hallway; living room on right, bedroom on the
>   left, kitchen in back
> the house has only one bathroom; gym in the basement

DÉCOR AND CONSTRUCTION

Décor describes how interiors look and what they contain and are made of: color, style, and composition of walls, fixtures, and drapery; color, style, and placement of furniture; utilities and other technology; and other appearance and functional details. Watch for (and query) fixtures or décor that seem out of place (such as an electric stove in a shanty in the middle of nowhere).

a green velvet sofa under the window
creaky wooden floors; an old screen door
dark paneled walls
kitchen island with a marble counter and gas cooktop
Betty's home office has a business landline; horizontal filing
    cabinets; barrister bookcases

RIGHT/LEFT DISTINCTIONS

On which side of the hallway is Angelina's bedroom? Which way do you turn when you get off the elevator to get to the executive suite? Record mentions of right and left for locations of objects or movement through an interior space.

the main staircase turns to the right
Raphael's office is on the left side of the hallway off the
    living room

NUMBER OF STORIES

Floor levels can be tricky to describe. A common point of confusion is the fact that (for example) the *fourth* floor is up *three* flights of stairs (but also see the last paragraph in this section). (Think about it: the second floor is up one flight, the third floor is up two flights, and so on.) You can allow a fudge factor for higher floors; what's one floor more or less if you're on the thirtieth floor? Let Karen say that she hauled herself up thirty flights of stairs because the elevator was broken. But for less than, say, ten floors, it makes a difference. Let the context be your guide.

The same rule applies for going down. If someone jumps (or is thrown!) out a fourth-floor window, they fall only three floors (assuming they land on the ground and not on an awning or balcony).

When you record the number of floors in a structure, assume nothing. If an apartment is on the third floor, the most you can deduce is that the building has *at least* three floors—not that it has *only* three floors. And in some residential buildings in New York City, the "ground" (or sometimes "garden") level is a few steps below the street, and the first floor is up a flight of steps.

Finally, watch out when describing floor numbers in a British context or in dialogue from a British character. In American usage, the floor at street level is the *first floor*, whereas in British usage, the same floor is the *ground floor*, the floor above that is the *first floor*, and so on. You may need to leave yourself notes on such references to be sure that they align with each other.

What if you find a contradiction?

See chapter 4 for guidance on resolving discrepancies. If there is a minor difference, you can change and query. But if the problem involves a factor that's critical to the plot, bring it to the author's attention and suggest solutions if you can.

Watch for things that, though consistent, don't seem right, either logically or aesthetically. Why is the living room ultramodern but the kitchen rustic? Why do different rooms in different houses have nearly identical décor? How can Mirax open a window of her habitat pod to let in the hot Drashi breeze, if she has to wear an atmo suit to go outside? Always picture the scene and ask yourself if it makes sense.

PLACES
Fabulous Author, *Contemporary Series Romance*

Note: PB denotes information from *Previous Book.*
(?) = queried in ms.

PLEASANTVILLE, WYOMING	(Ch. #)
on a plateau between two mountain ridges to the east and west	PB
founded in 1875; population 5,200	PB
county seat; has 2 stoplights	PB
Big Rock River—winds through southern WY; includes **Big Rock Falls**	PB

Miguel Torres's ranch	
in a valley; 10 miles from the city limits; 8 miles from the feed mill; over 500 acres	PB, 1
driveway is a graveled road; cedars on each side	PB
living room to the right of the hallway, dining room to the left, kitchen in back	PB
bedrooms and bathroom upstairs	PB
Miguel's study is downstairs; leather armchair, large desk piled with books	24
red siding; wraparound porch; weathered shutters	32

Eldon Russell's homestead	
close to the county line; 4 miles from the fire station (?)	1, 6, 7
small cabin with a loft; surrounded by aspen trees	3, 25, 29
small garage/workshop	28

Hunter Ford's house	
big old farmhouse on the edge of town; 3 stories	PB, 19
large sunny kitchen with an island and rustic cabinets	PB
Hunter's suite is on the top floor; Jennie's room is on the 2nd floor	PB, 18
large double doors open onto the porch; paved driveway	19

Louise (?) and Genie Simpson's apartment	
run-down building downtown; rickety outdoor stairs; on the 2nd floor in the back	46

Louis's (?) office	
on the 3rd floor of **City Hall**	3
waiting area: upholstered chairs, coffee table, red area rug	3
office: large wooden desk with computer, 2 old file cabinets, leather chair	3
private bathroom	3

Figure 5.1. Sample style sheet: places (descriptive entries on separate lines)

bakery—closes at 8 pm on weekdays 3
Big Sky Diner—on the square; open 24/7 PB
Bucky's Roadhouse—next to the hotel PB
Country Kettle—on the western edge of town PB, P
Ella's Ice Cream PB
First Baptist Church PB
general store—on Main Street, a block from the square PB
library—story hour on Wednesday mornings 7, 32
Old West Museum—downtown PB
Pump 'n' Go—gas station; newly rebuilt PB
the Pizza Pit PB

Main Street PB, 2
Foxhound Road 4

Yarrow Creek 9
White Feather Ridge 9
Southern Wyoming University PB

CROOKED SPRINGS

has a drive-in theater, shopping mall, small airport 5

LONELY MOOSE RESORT

in Colorado, about 175 miles from Pleasantville PB

Note: (##) = chapter number; PB denotes information from *Previous Book.*
(?) = queried in ms.

PLEASANTVILLE, WYOMING: on a plateau between two mountain ridges to the east and
 west, founded in 1875, population 5,200, county seat; has 2 stoplights (PB)
Big Rock River: winds through southern WY, includes **Big Rock Falls** (PB)

Miguel Torres's ranch: in a valley, 10 miles from the city limits, 8 miles from the feed mill,
 over 500 acres (PB, 1); driveway is a graveled road, cedars on each side (PB); living
 room to the right of the hallway, dining room to the left, kitchen in back (PB); bedrooms
 and bathroom upstairs (PB) Miguel's study is downstairs: leather armchair, large desk
 piled with books (24); red siding, wraparound porch, weathered shutters (32)
Eldon Russell's homestead: close to the county line (1) 4 miles from the fire station (?) (6, 7);
 small cabin with loft, surrounded by aspen trees (3, 25, 29); small garage/workshop (28)
Hunter Ford's house: big old farmhouse, edge of town (PB); 3 stories (19) large sunny kitchen
 with an island and rustic cabinets (PB); Hunter's suite is on the top floor (PB); Jennie's
 room on the 2nd floor (18); large double doors open onto the porch; paved driveway (19)
Louise (?) and Genie Simpson's apartment: run-down building downtown; rickety outdoor
 stairs; on the 2nd floor in the back (46)
Louis's (?) office: 3rd floor, **City Hall;** waiting area: upholstered chairs, coffee table, red rug;
 office: large wooden desk w/computer, 2 old file cabinets, leather chair; private bath (3)

bakery: closes at 8 pm on weekdays (3)
Big Sky Diner: on the square; open 24/7 (PB)
Bucky's Roadhouse: next to the hotel (PB)
Country Kettle: on the western edge of town (PB)
Ella's Ice Cream (PB)
First Baptist Church (PB)
general store: on Main Street, a block from the square (PB)
library: story hour on Wednesday mornings (7, 32)
Old West Museum: downtown (PB)
Pump 'n' Go: gas station; newly rebuilt (PB)
the Pizza Pit (PB)

Main Street (PB, 2)
Foxhound Road (4)

Yarrow Creek (9)
White Feather Ridge (9)
Southern Wyoming University (PB)

CROOKED SPRINGS: has a drive-in theater, shopping mall, small airport (5)

LONELY MOOSE RESORT: in Colorado, about 175 miles from Pleasantville (PB)

Figure 5.2. Sample style sheet: places (descriptive entries run-in)

6

Timeline

The timeline of the story must be kept consistent with its fictional world and sometimes with actual events in the real world. Authors often have difficulty maintaining a consistent timeline. Good thing you've got their back!

Always create a timeline, whether you think you will need one or not. You may be surprised by the number of time references in the story, and at least a few discrepancies usually reveal themselves. I can think of only a few manuscripts I've copyedited in which the passage of time was so vague or such a nonessential part of the plot that a timeline was not needed or could not be created. Even if there are no specific references to days, years, seasons, and so on, events usually occur in a certain order. And when the author has given extremely detailed time markers, it's important to cross-check them all for accuracy.

Let's look at some methods for keeping the timeline on track.

Layout

I seldom see timelines created by others, whether created by the copyeditor of a previous book in a series or provided by the author. (So if you create one, you're already a rock star!) They are usually in a straight text format: paragraphs or a bulleted list beginning with "Day One" or "Monday, September 3." Occasionally it's more of a plot outline, by chapter. This format works well for simple, linear timelines with little detail such as specific times or days of the week or relative time references (*one day* rather than *four days later*). Historical fiction (particularly medieval and earlier) and speculative fiction (days have little meaning in space, and a fantasy world may not have names for days and months) are good candidates for this type of timeline (see figure 6.1).

However, if the story contains a lot of specific references to time, plot-critical events happening on certain days, recurring events happening on certain days or at certain times, flashbacks, characters on different timelines, and other complex configurations, a visual format may be more helpful. I'm a visual thinker when it comes to time and calendars, and most of the manuscripts I copyedit are fairly specific about time, so I lay out my timeline as a Word table that's set up like a monthly calendar (see figure 6.2). It has a header row with the days of the week, and the weeks extend for as long as the story lasts. (Long, empty swaths of time are indicated with a single blank row and a notation such as SIX MONTHS LATER, rather than twenty-six empty rows.) This makes it easy to spot when, for example, a school day falls on a weekend or there are only two weeks between the first buds of spring and the midsummer festival.

To begin filling in a calendar-style timeline, start your notes on any day in the first row. If the first paragraph begins on a Wednesday, great! Start your notes there. If not, just pick a day and record the progression of time as you go. You might pick Monday as your starting day, but then chapter 3, two days later, might be Friday; now you know that you need to move your calendar entries for chapters 1 and 2 forward two days. If there's a flashback to five years ago in chapter 7, add blank rows as needed above the start of your timeline to accommodate it. And so on.

Details to track

Record any references to time, specific or relative. Occasionally the author includes time indicators as heads in the text, often at the beginning of each chapter: *Friday night* or *March 26*. Great! On the timeline they go. Specific time markers can be a help (if they turn out to be accurate) or a hindrance (if they don't). Record the chapter number (if provided) where each mention of a timeline element appears. See figure 6.2 for examples.

ANY MENTION OF TIME: FIXED, RELATIVE, RECURRING

Time references can sneak right past you until you get used to catching them. References to specific times, days, months, and so on are easy to spot (it's five thirty in the morning!; the bar was pretty empty for a Saturday; a hot August night). Other clues to time are a bit more subtle (the first rays of the sun; rush hour; midterms; the week of Martinmas).

Time references can also be relative to each other (three days later; after six weeks of sailing lessons) or recurring (Garun shifts at the full moon; Thursday night darts league). Check that *three days later* makes sense in context; that the sailing lessons aren't in the dead of winter when the lake is frozen over; that Garun shifts every four weeks, when the moon is full; and that the darts league doesn't end up on Saturday night (without an explanation), replaced with some other activity (without explanation), or forgotten altogether (if its absence is noticeable; for example, if the big tournament is next week but never happens).

WEATHER, SUN POSITION, MOON PHASES, AND SEASONS

Both static moments and the passage of time can be indicated by the state of the environment. What's the weather doing? (If it was snowing an hour ago, we know both the season and that people are probably wearing warm clothes outside.) Where is the sun? (The sun's position in the sky tells us the approximate time of day.) What is the current phase of the moon? (A full moon can be romantic, or foreboding, or it can illuminate a night scene, but you can't have a full moon every night for two weeks in a row.) Seasons can be indicated by an outright statement (a warm autumn afternoon) or hinted at (the maple trees shone gold in the sunshine).

SCHOOL DAYS, WORKDAYS

Another subtle way of marking time is things that happen on certain days. Students generally attend school on weekdays; the same principle holds for office workers. Religious events and holidays fall on certain days of the week or specific dates. Check those references against your timeline. This is where tracking relative mentions of time comes in. If a scene takes place on a Thursday, and then three days later Harriet gets in trouble at school, that should raise a red flag. And if Jasper, who works a nine-to-five job, is in the office along with all of his coworkers on a Saturday afternoon, business as usual, that's a good time to query as well.

> "No video games on a school night!"
> the bustle of morning commuters
> George travels for work, is only home on weekends

CRITICAL PLOT EVENTS

Recording the day on which an important event happens (Charles's accident) gives you something to refer to later (two weeks after the accident), even if the specific day is not mentioned. Conversely, if an event is supposed to happen on a certain day (the auction is a week from Friday), make sure that the plot progresses so that it actually happens on that day (not on a Wednesday three weeks from now). And make sure that it happens at all, and if not, that there's a reason why. If not, it's time for a query.

CHARACTER AGES/BIRTHDAYS

Character ages often get out of whack, especially when the story takes place over years or decades, or if there are many references to ages relative to other characters. Your first pass will tell you how to approach this. If the story takes place over a few days, weeks, or months, ages are likely to have little relevance to the plot and don't need to go on the timeline. Instead, just record the age in the character's entry instead of on the timeline:

> age 38
> in her late 60s

Pay attention to indirect references to ages and birthdays, which can tell you a lot. For example, suppose Ada says I had just turned thirty-six. You know her age, and you may also know the month or the time of year. If it's now June, then Ada's birthday is probably in May or early June. So you can add her age under her character description (age 36; birthday is probably in May/early June, with chapter number, if provided) and also a note on the timeline to show when her birthday falls in the overall plot. Then you have something to check when other age references appear; if Ada turned thirty-six in June, then she can't be thirty-seven in October, and thirty-nine the next summer.

Other clues to ages include life phases: grades in school (a seventh grader is probably age twelve or thirteen), physical and mental development (losing baby teeth, speech development, reaching puberty), graduation from high school and higher education, and retirement.

Relative ages of characters also come into play. If two siblings are three years apart in age, make sure they stay that way by reviewing other clues or statements about their ages. If the characters consist of a large family spanning several generations, make sure the ages work; for example, if Moira is seventy-five but her granddaughter is forty-five, unless both Moira and her child were teenage parents, something is wrong. If things get really complicated, drawing a family tree might help.

Why is it important to record these details? Disparate pieces of information need to tie together. For example, it traditionally takes seven years to become a lawyer (although some accelerated programs make it possible in a shorter time frame). However, a practicing lawyer who's twenty-two years old might be a stretch, and thus worth a query. There's often room for flexibility, especially when fixed and relative ages aren't critical to the plot, but it's wise to query large discrepancies and suggest fixes if you can.

> Cole was born last fall
> a decade older than Lina
> when we were both in seventh grade

HISTORICAL EVENTS, ACTUAL DATES

Occasionally the plot hinges on real historical events, or the manuscript includes date heads with the day of the week, month, and year. Check those dates! Query if there are mentions of the day of the week that do not align with the actual dates. An online perpetual calendar such as the one at timeanddate.com can help; some calendars also include holidays. Some authors don't care whether their historical events, especially very old ones, align with the actual calendar for that date, and that's fine. But a query is still needed.

Here's an example of the detective work you might do: Suppose that chapter 1 begins the story in April 1925. Then in chapter 4 we learn that the ladies' social club meets monthly. Then in chapter 5, the meeting takes place, as always, on the second Wednesday, on a bright April evening. Boom! You have enough information to look up the date (Wednesday, April 8, 1925). (You also know to confirm that later meetings are also on the second Wednesday of the month.)

Some authors of historical fiction deliberately fictionalize dates or events for the purposes of their story. The reasons for this are often discussed in an afterword. If a variance from historical fact is not explicitly explained, write a tactful query noting the discrepancy and asking if it's intentional. (See also the section titled "Anachronisms of both fact and language" in chapter 9.)

FICTIONAL TIME DIVISIONS

In speculative fiction, you may encounter worlds in which days or months have fictional names or are divided strangely (for example, nine-day weeks and twenty-five-day months). Or each day might be divided into fifteen hours, which have names instead of numbers. Record these facts under general style and on your timeline.

Days of the week may not have names at all in stories that are set in invented worlds or far in the past; if you use a calendar-based timeline, change your column heads from *Sunday* through *Saturday* to generic terms such as *Weekday 1* through *Weekday 7* (or however many days the weeks have). If you copyedit such manuscripts frequently, consider creating a separate timeline template (see Appendix A: Style Sheet Templates) to avoid reinventing the wheel for each project.

SLACK TIME (INDETERMINATE SPANS OF TIME)

Time references are often vague (a few days later; one afternoon). In such cases, I simply take my best guess as to where to place it in the timeline table. *A few days later* might be two or three days, so just place it two or three days later for now; you can always move it later if new information comes to light. You can use other clues, such as whether it's a weekday (judging by school days or business hours) or phrases like *later this week* (unlikely if today is Saturday). If your timeline includes days that are not specific (for example, a day that is listed under Tuesday may not be specifically identified as Tuesday in the text), include a note to that effect at the top of the table. The phrasing I use is Days of the week are best estimates except where specified as in the manuscript.

Also, check whether the way characters speak about the passage of time makes sense. If not, you may need to revisit the timeline, flag the passage for review later, or insert a query. Consider the following situations:

- When it's Wednesday and Sharon says, *"I can't, I've got that meeting on Wednesday."* (Does she mean to say "later today" or "next Wednesday," or is today not really Wednesday?)
- When it's Friday and Yusuf says, *"I'll get back to you later this week."* (There's only one day left in the week; does he mean "tomorrow" or "next week"?)
- When it's Monday and Veronica says, *"This has been the week from hell!"* (referring to events that began four days ago). (It's Monday, so the week has barely started, and most of the events took place last week. There's wiggle room here, as people sometimes use the word *week* to mean the previous seven days instead of a calendar week, but still it's good to query if the usage is particularly odd in context.)

SCENE BREAKS

Not all *scene breaks* (clearly delineated breaks or gaps in the action) are created equal. Some are indicated in so many words: five hours later, Wednesday night, July 17. Others are less clear: one fine morning, the days melted into weeks—or there may be a new scene with no indication at all of how much time has passed. And either type may or may not be marked with a visual break, such as a *space break* with or without an ornament. So it's useful to record on your timeline where scene breaks occur, in case a scene or a chunk of time needs to be moved on your timeline (perhaps along with scenes that follow or precede it), a time reference needs to be changed, or there is a question about exactly when an event happened, if the description is vague.

You might simply add something like <scene break> to your timeline. I insert a graphic element in my timeline table to indicate a scene break, with an explanatory note at the top of the table (see figure 6.2). Whatever notation you use, make it stand out so you and future users of your style sheet can see where the breaks are, in case they need to be adjusted.

CHANGES IN POINT OF VIEW
In addition to breaks in time or place, changes in point of view from one character to another often provide scene breaks. It can help to insert the point-of-view character's name on your timeline at the beginning of each point-of-view scene change (see figure 6.2). In a complex plot with elements such as multiple, constantly changing points of view or parallel timelines, indicating changes in point of view will be quite useful.

PARALLEL TIMELINES AND FLASHBACKS
Occasionally characters move in parallel timelines. Perhaps they have separated and are journeying in different directions (or are moving toward each other). For example, odd-numbered chapters might be about Matthew, who's on the run from the law, while the even-numbered chapters are about the people who are looking for him.

You'll need to devise a way to distinguish the two (or more!) paths. Perhaps each gets its own row in a timeline table, with bold text or a tint distinguishing one path from the other. On a text-based timeline, you might set one path indented and bold and the other flush left and roman.

Parallel timelines can be tricky. It's awkward when time jumps backward and forward between the two (or more) paths. Another common problem occurs when two groups of characters diverge for several chapters, but when they are reunited, the same amount of time has not passed for both. These types of issues can be difficult to resolve without rewriting; a simple query to the author explaining the problem may be the best you can do, unless you can suggest an easy fix.

Some stories have flashbacks, time travel, or sections of the plot taking place in different years or across decades, such as when the main story is in the present day but an important part of the plot has occurred several decades earlier, perhaps when the main character was a child. It's helpful to separate these larger chunks of time for clarity. In my timeline table, I insert a blank horizontal shaded row and perhaps a line or two of explanatory text, such as the year or location, if the location differs from the other sections (see figure 6.2).

TIME ZONES AND TRAVEL TIMES

Some plots involve concurrent action at different points around the world, travel from one part of the planet to another, and so on. For example, suppose Rebecca in New York City is having lunch and calls Ewan in London, waking him before dawn. She asks him to complete several tasks before leaving Heathrow at noon London time to arrive in New York City just in time for the big finale at midnight. And these events and times are all critical to the plot.

This is impossible: New York is five hours behind London, not ahead, so lunchtime in New York is late afternoon in London, not early morning. And a noon flight from London would arrive in New York around 2:30 p.m. New York time, not midnight.

When you're checking separate timelines and travel times, make sure that the time zone differences add up. Look up flight duration times as well as local time for takeoff and landing.

MISSING ELEMENTS

Watch for "missing" holidays and big events such as milestone birthdays, if their absence is remarkable; what constitutes "remarkable" depends on the genre. The following are some example scenarios you might encounter:

- In a military thriller, the main-character assassin may not be concerned about celebrating his fiftieth birthday, but in a homey arts-and-crafts-themed romance novel or cozy mystery, it would be unusual for the Christmas season to pass without comment.

- If a character has a major event coming up (for example, a big meeting at work or an important recital), check to make sure that the event happens. If it doesn't happen, is the omission explained?
- Pay attention to holidays when businesses, offices, schools, and other facilities shouldn't be open. For example, the bank should not be open on July 1 (Canada Day) in Canada.

What if I find a contradiction?

Look for logical inconsistencies relating to the passage of time. If a group of soldiers takes more than a month to march a hundred miles over fairly flat terrain (less than three miles a day), that seems unusually slow, and it's query time. If Hugo left his room at eight p.m., *the hours passed*, and then it was nine p.m., either it's much later now, or less time than *hours* has passed. An event that was in the timeline three months ago would likely not be referred to as "the other day."

Sometimes you can fix timeline discrepancies by adjusting vague references (such as changing *three weeks later* to *two weeks later*, if making that change does not disrupt other elements) and writing a query to ask the author to confirm. Or you might change *Thursday* to *Friday* and query. But you must be certain that you are not introducing another error. In other cases, the problem is too convoluted for a simple fix. In that case, write an explanatory query, make suggestions if you can, and let the author handle it. You can also flag the problem areas on your timeline with highlighting or table cell shading and refer to this in your query to illustrate what isn't working and why.

It may take some practice and experience to tune your attention to the sometimes vague and subtle references to time while copyediting a work of fiction. But your authors will thank you for it!

TIMELINE

**twelve years ago: Parker was 17 and Ana was 16**

Parker is failing math; Ana tries to tutor him but he won't take it seriously and keeps teasing her (and has a secret crush on her) [...]

**Sunday, August 3, early morning**

Chapter 1
Ana being kept awake by banging in the hotel, goes out into the hall to find out where it's coming from
A half-naked Parker bursts out into the hall from his room as Ana is walking by, startling her
Parker realizes Ana is flustered and that he still has a thing for her
maintenance man comes out of the room across the hall and breaks the charged moment

Chapter 2
later that morning: Ana, Rosalia, and Lily meet in the hotel restaurant for brunch
Parker and Brandon come in; Parker notices Ana
Frank and Carolyn tell Parker they want to move to Florida and have Parker take over the day-to-day management of the vineyard
Parker realizes he needs help getting up to speed with math so he can run the vineyard, asks Ana if she'd consider helping him like she used to

**unknown day that week**

Chapter 3
Ana and Rosalia have drinks after work, discuss Ana's lack of date prospects for Brianne's upcoming wedding [...]

**Saturday, August 9**

Chapter 6
Donna sees Parker arriving at Ana's house, gets nosy and corners him
Ana comes outside; Parker acts like it's a date to prevent Ana from telling Donna that he's getting tutoring
Ana is inspired to get Parker to agree to be her date for Brianne's wedding
Ana and Parker agree that she will tutor him in exchange for him being her "boyfriend" for the next six weeks. [...]

**Wednesday, August 13**

[second tutoring session] [...]

Figure 6.1. Sample style sheet: timeline (text-based)

TIMELINE—Fabulous Author, *Contemporary Series Romance*

Notes: days of the week are best estimates except where specified as in the ms.

"———//———" indicates scene/time break

(?) indicates something that has been queried in ms.

SUNDAY	MONDAY	TUESDAY	WEDNESDAY	THURSDAY	FRIDAY	SATURDAY
	KAREN (Prologue) story begins; midnight; raining					
		MIGUEL (Ch. 1) May 4; sunset / (2) midnight; the sheriff arrives	(3) next day / (3) 6 pm	(3) 4 am / (3) 11 am		(3) 2 days later; Sam goes out of town
	KAREN (4) May 10; 2 pm / MIGUEL (5) 9:15 pm; Sam has returned; calls Miguel	(5) May 11 / (5) midafternoon / (5) past 11 pm; full moon (?)	(6) 2 am / ———//——— / KAREN (7) May 12, lunchtime	(7) next morning	(7) Friday night; water main breaks	
MIGUEL (8) almost 2 weeks have passed since Miguel received the letter / (8) Sunday morning 10 am	(8) next day; Sam returns		KAREN (9) May 19 / (9) sunny; 9 am / (9) lunch / (10) dusk	(11) May 20; Karen and James stop in at the hotel	(12) next day	
(12) May 23; noon / (12) Karen and James go on a picnic; they fight		MIGUEL (13) May 25; Clayton has the flu / (13) midnight; full moon (?)	(13) next day / (13) book club rescheduled for next Tuesday (?) / KAREN (14) May 26, moonless night	(14) next morning; 4 days after the fight; Karen and James make up	(14) next day; Janet hires Karen to help / (14) 9:30 pm; barn fire	(15) May 29; barn fire article in the *Gazette* (?)

Sample Style Sheet—Timeline, page 1 of 2

Figure 6.2. Sample style sheet: timeline (calendar-based)

TIMELINE—Fabulous Author, *Contemporary Series Romance*

SUNDAY	MONDAY	TUESDAY	WEDNESDAY	THURSDAY	FRIDAY	SATURDAY
MIGUEL (16) next morning; 8 am	(17) May 31; 5:15 pm (?) (17) Johnny injured (18) 11:45 pm	(19) 1 am ——//—— KAREN (20) June 1; 9 am	(22) June 2 (22) Maggie's close call was 3 months ago ——//—— (23) June 2; afternoon ——//—— (23) June 2; 11:30 pm	(24) June 3; Quinn and Karen go to Crooked Springs	(25) next morning; last day of school ——//—— MIGUEL (26) party at Miguel's ranch tomorrow night	(26) June 5 (26) 3 weeks since the water main break (26) party; James and Mitchell fight (26) Johnny wakes up
	(27) June 7; Monday morning (27) the crew visits Johnny	KAREN (28) June 8; Sparky is missing (29) dinnertime	(30) 6:15 am (31) Sparky returns (32) June 9; bedtime	(32) next morning; 10:30 am	MIGUEL (33) June 11, 2 pm (34) Quinn goes to Miguel's for dinner ——//—— KAREN (35) James talks to Karen	(36) Saturday morning, June 12 MIGUEL (37) 9:30 am (38) Johnny was injured 2 weeks ago
	(39) June 14; midmorning (39) 2 weeks after the fire	(40) June 15; morning; Johnny goes home	KAREN (42) June 16 (42) storm (42) 11 pm	(43) 2:37 am (44) dawn the next day		
				MIGUEL (48) 2 weeks later		
TWO MONTHS LATER					KAREN (49) a sunny Friday afternoon	

Part III
Editorial Issues Specific to Fiction

Many basic copyediting concepts apply to both fiction and nonfiction, but a different mindset is needed when copyediting fiction. As discussed in part I, fiction entertains more than it informs, and to that end, the rules of formal English are often intentionally relaxed or broken. In addition, many elements of fiction tend to be scarce in nonfiction: point of view, adult themes, dialogue, slang and dialect, and the balance between real and unreal, to name a few broad categories. Conscious language is an important factor in both, however, and the fiction copyeditor must also watch out for unnecessarily biased language and inappropriate representation of characters and situations.

This final part moves away from the logistics of copyediting fiction to discuss general elements that are particularly associated with fiction: relaxing the rules of grammar and usage, copyediting dialogue, and blending real-world facts with fiction.

7

Grammar and Usage in Fiction

Grammar and style are much more informal and even cutting-edge in fiction than in nonfiction, particularly in dialogue and first-person narration. This chapter begins with a discussion of point of view, verb tenses, and narrative distance and the copyeditor's role in keeping them in line. Next up is language bloopers: learning to spot infelicities of language (such as dangling modifiers, nonparallel construction, and pet phrases) and when to fix them, query them, or leave them alone. The final sections of the chapter are devoted to profanity and sexual terms, conscious language, and copyediting the English spoken and written in different countries.

Here are some examples of notations of casual application of grammar and usage that might appear in the usage section of your style sheet:

- Allow singular *they/them/themself*

  Singular *they* is gaining traction even in formal writing and is increasingly accepted and recommended by standard dictionaries and style manuals.

- Allow informal use of the subjunctive (I wish I was dead)

  Some authors distinguish between using the formal subjunctive form for truly impossible situations (his head felt as if it were ten feet wide) and informal subjunctive for possible or probable situations (she shivered, as if she was chilled).

- Allow misplaced *either/only* (I only have five dollars)
- OK to ignore *who/whom* distinction (Who are you talking to?)

The *who/whom* rule is losing ground, particularly in fiction and especially in dialogue. Many experienced editors have trouble determining when to use *who* or *whom*, and most English speakers don't observe the distinction when they talk. However, it can be perfectly fine to apply this "rule" inconsistently—for example, by following it in third-person narration but ignoring it in dialogue; following it in adult dialogue but not for children's dialogue (have you ever met a kid who says *whom*?), or following it for a character who's highly educated and speaks in formal, stilted language and ignoring it for characters who speak more naturally and casually.

- Comma splices OK (I heard what you said, I'm not going!)

Some authors and publishers dislike semicolons in fiction, particularly in dialogue; the feeling is that they are too formal or that "people don't speak semicolons." These manuscripts are more likely to contain comma splices. Other authors allow comma splices in dialogue, but not in narration. In fiction, comma splices often factor into pacing and voice. Unless the comma splice creates a problem such as confusion, ambiguity, or a garden-path sentence (discussed shortly), it's fine to stet. However, if comma splices are so prevalent as to be distracting, it may be a good idea to eliminate a few (or ask the author to do so).

- Sentence fragments OK (She couldn't breathe. Gasping. No air. Blacking out. *Don't panic! Don't! Don't! Don't!*)

Just like comma splices, sentence fragments abound in fiction. They are how people talk. They are used for pacing, or drama, or character voice. They are perfectly acceptable.

Point of view and verb tenses

Fiction authors choose from a variety of points of view, and often they switch point of view from chapter to chapter; each chapter might be from a different character's point of view, whether alternating between two main characters or among three or more. In addition, a variety of verb tenses may be used for narration. Most fiction is written in simple past tense (*Rex glanced at his watch*); however, present tense conveys a sense of both intimacy and immediacy (*I shake my head and try again*). Your job as copyeditor is to ensure consistency and clarity in whatever point of view and tense the author has chosen.

POINT OF VIEW

Ensure that point of view is represented consistently and that transitions of point of view between characters are clearly delineated. Sometimes the point of view changes by chapter. Within chapters, space breaks or even chapter subheads indicate changes in point of

Narrative Distance

Narrative distance describes the extent to which the reader is invited into the narrator's head and into the story. Narrative distance is closer when the narrator directly addresses the reader (*Do you know what I mean?*) and further away when they do not. It's closer when the narrator uses terms like *this* and *here* and *tomorrow* to describe time and place, and further away when they use terms like *that* and *there* and *the next day*. Similar pairs denoting closer vs. further narrative distance include *these/those, this afternoon/that afternoon, tonight/ that night, yesterday/the day before*, and *a year ago/a year earlier*. See Beth Hill's blog at http://theeditorsblog.net for an extensive discussion of narrative distance.

Generally authors choose their narrative distance with care, even varying it among scenes or character points of view, and copyeditors should leave it alone. However, watch for passages where narrative distance has inadvertently slipped from one form to another, perhaps as part of the revision process. Let the overall tone of the manuscript be your guide.

view; context clues in the first sentence or two after the change also do the trick. If you find yourself going back to reread a passage because you thought it was a different character's voice, it's time to insert a query alerting the author to the problem.

Also be aware of *head-hopping*, which occurs when the point of view changes or alternates quickly between two or more characters' viewpoints (seeing through their eyes, hearing their thoughts, feeling their feelings) without a scene break. This practice is generally frowned on, although occasionally it can be done well. But most of the time it just confuses readers. Sometimes it can be remedied by changing a word or two, with a query to the author explaining why. For example, in a passage that is *not* in Clara's point of view, you could suggest changing "I can see that," Clara said, worried about how he would react. to "I can see that." Clara seemed worried about how he would react. This changes the point of view from how Clara herself *feels* to how she *appears* to the other person. But if the problem would require more work, simply query and leave any recasting to the author. (See also the sidebar titled "Narrative Distance" for a related discussion.)

VERB TENSES

Past tense/present tense: Past tense is, in my opinion, the easiest narrative tense to edit because it's how we naturally tell a story, whether in first person (I strolled down to the corner) or third person (Quill shouted, "Wait!"), so problematic present-tense verbs tend to be easy to spot. Copyediting present tense can be trickier because our minds are conditioned to expect past tense in storytelling, so if an errant past-tense verb slips into present-tense narration, we often pass right over it without noticing that it's out of place. Read carefully when copyediting present-tense narration and inspect the verbs closely—particularly dialogue tags (*said* vs. *says*), which are a popular breeding ground for tense errors because when they are well done they tend to "disappear."

Past tense/past perfect tense: Another common error occurs in past-tense narration when action occurs in the past of the story, but the past perfect tense (what I like to think of as "super past") isn't used to indicate it. Most often the problem is a missing *had* (with an appropriate change in the main verb form):

> I tiptoed into the room, which was obviously ransacked before I arrived. (past tense only)

> I tiptoed into the room, which had obviously been ransacked before I arrived. (past tense followed by past perfect, to indicate prior action)

Past perfect indicating the "past of the past" usually provides an effective signpost that something happened before the current action. However, it isn't always necessary and can be intrusive, particularly in long flashback passages. These are often indicated with a sentence or two in past perfect to establish the "super past," and then the flashback continues in simple past tense. After the flashback, context brings the reader back to the current story:

> She recalled the night she discovered the truth. Fall had come early that year, and the trees were almost bare. [flashback continues in simple past . . .]
>
> A branch scraping against the window snapped her out of her reverie. The truth didn't matter anymore.

See Carol Saller's post about flashbacks and the past perfect at the *CMOS Shop Talk* blog for more information.

Cutting deadwood

Sometimes extra words serve creative purposes—but other times they're unnecessary. In nonfiction, tightening up the prose is practically automatic, but in fiction, tread carefully. You can often help the author remove deadwood—but be mindful of voice and especially rhythm, and be especially cautious when copyediting dialogue. When in doubt, query rather than editing outright (especially when copyediting for a publisher, as these constructions may have already been discussed). Here are a few examples:

- *There is/are/were; It is/was:* Phrases beginning with *there is*, *it was*, *this is an X that is Y*, and similar constructions are sometimes awkward and unnecessary circumlocutions. Scrutinize them closely, especially in narration, and see if they can be made more concise without altering the voice.

"There's no way I'm going in there!" (fine as is; dialogue, character's voice)

There was a man who stood in the corner, smoking a cigarette. (simple description; consider suggesting A man stood)

- *Smothered verbs:* A *smothered verb* is a verb that has been turned into a noun: *made a decision* (*decided*), *came to a conclusion* (*concluded*), *have a tendency* (*tend*). Smothered verbs can usually be turned back into actual verbs (with an explanatory query), but consider the context.

I'd made my decision, and I knew it was the right one. (fine as is; the noun form is needed here)

After college, he'd made a decision to travel around China for a year. (simple statement; consider suggesting he'd decided)

- *Redundant body parts and other words:* What else would you nod except your head? Can you blink anything but your eyes? And if you can shrug your knee, I'd love a demonstration. In simple phrases like *nodded her head, blinked* (or *squinted*) *their eyes*, or *shrugged his shoulders*, you can usually safely amputate the extraneous body part: *she nodded, they blinked, he shrugged*. On the other hand, context may dictate that it should remain—for example, if the body part is preceded by an adjective (*he shrugged one shoulder*) or if the full phrase is part of the rhythm of the entire sentence (*The children simply could not stop moving: nodding their heads, tapping their feet, waving their arms*). Autonomous body parts (particularly eyes) and redundant descriptions can also be a problem:

Her eyes bounced around the room.

His eyes grabbed her and refused to let go.

His feet trudged down the street.

My ears heard the click of the lock.

Her hands flopped uselessly at the ends of her arms.

Not only do body parts sometimes act on their own, but metaphors and clichés can create ridiculous mental images. Edit and query accordingly.

Words other than body parts are also sometimes candidates for the ax. Unless we're talking about telepathic communication, people don't think to anyone but themselves; phrases like *she thought* can sometimes be deleted, if italics or other context makes it clear that she is thinking that thought. (See the section titled "Unspoken dialogue" in chapter 8 for further discussion of how to style thoughts.)

- *Extraneous adverbs:* Mark Twain famously advised writers to "substitute 'damn' every time you're inclined to write 'very'; your editor will delete it and the writing will be just as it should be." Proceed with caution; don't go on a search-and-destroy mission. Adverbs like *very, totally, actually, just,* and *really* are often used for emphasis, emotion, rhythm, and the like, especially in dialogue and first-person narration. But consider whether the sentence might be stronger without them and worth a query to the author to suggest deleting.

Language bloopers

In fiction, words are often used to paint a picture, but sometimes that image goes off the rails. (For example, in badly mixed metaphors like that one.) Authors sometimes have little writing habits that they don't notice, and wording and phrasing choices sometimes lead to inadvertent sound effects, ridiculous literal images, or syntactical dead ends. Let's look at some of these.

DANGLING AND MISPLACED MODIFIERS

The Copyeditor's Handbook includes an excellent discussion of dangling and misplaced modifiers and how to correct them. Although the milder versions often work fine in fiction (under the "that's how people talk" rule), it's good to develop the ability to spot them and consider whether they should be modified or queried.

NONPARALLEL CONSTRUCTION

Nonparallel construction turns up regularly in natural speech ("that's how people talk"): You either did or you didn't. However, we must also consider the reader and whether the nonparallelism will pull them out of the story as they try to parse it. Here's a common example:

> Elinor poured and handed a cup of tea to the duchess. (awkward; she didn't pour a cup of tea *to* the duchess)

> Elinor poured a cup of tea and handed it to the duchess. (better)

See *The Copyeditor's Handbook* for a great explanation of various nonparallel constructions and how to fix them.

MIXED METAPHORS

Like dangling and misplaced modifiers, mixed metaphors often produce a humorous, nonsensical mental image.

> Let's bury the past and begin with a clean slate.

> I could see the writing on the wall, and I needed to nip it in the bud.

In fiction, this can be deliberate—for example, if a character is being portrayed as confused or is making a joke. But sometimes a metaphor is a little bit *too* on point, so that it creates a pun. This may be intentional or inadvertent on the part of the author, and it never hurts to insert a query to ask in a case like this:

> The new gardener was getting to be a thorn in her side.

Pay close attention to metaphors when you encounter them, and query if you encounter a mixed metaphor or one that falls flat or doesn't make sense.

PET PHRASES

Pet phrases are little recurring bits of text or action, and often the author is unaware of them. Is everyone *shoving their hands through their hair* or *into their pockets*? *Sucking in a breath*? *Huffing a sigh*? *Trailing off* when they don't finish a sentence? Two or three occurrences probably aren't a big deal, but if you notice repeated phrases or actions as you edit, readers may notice as well and find it distracting.

Once you've identified a pet phrase, query it at the first occurrence; note the number of times it appears (you can also highlight each occurrence to illustrate the problem), and suggest revising a few of the problem phrases to reduce the repetition.

ALLITERATION, ASSONANCE, RHYME, AND ECHO

Edit with your ears as well as your eyes—not only because the story may be read aloud for an audiobook or by a screen reader, but also because the following types of "sound effects" may be unintentional. Check the context and query if they seem like they don't belong. (Is it an evocative description of a place or a memory? Or just a mundane list of the contents of a desk drawer?)

Alliteration occurs when the same sound appears at the beginning of several words or syllables in quick succession: *squelching through the sloppy, sludgy sewage.*

In general, *assonance* occurs when similar sounds are repeated in the middle of several words: *She was especially impressed by his pleasant expression.* (More specifically, *assonance* refers to repeated vowel sounds and *consonance* refers to repeated consonants; we'll use *assonance* to refer to both.)

Rhyme, for our purposes, is assonance at the ends of words (*I find that kind of refined speech attractive*) or phrases (*I can't say it more clearly; I loved her dearly*).

Echo covers a broader category of repetition, usually of whole words or parts of words, sometimes separated by a sentence or two: *He laid out the rug on the newly laid floor.* If it is unintentional or awkward, it is usually easily fixed by simple word substitution or slight recasting (with a query requesting approval).

GARDEN-PATH SENTENCES

Garden-path sentences are sneaky. Even though they are grammatically correct, they lead the reader to think the sentence is going one way ("down the garden path") when in fact it's going somewhere else, forcing the reader to backtrack to where the meaning went astray. Garden paths have several causes; here are a few examples:

- A missing *that* or *that was*: *I felt the blanket was too heavy.*
- A missing verb or transition word or phrase: *The man washed overboard sank under the waves.*
- Missing punctuation: *As Gorgan ran past the villagers gathered along the road cheered him on.*
- A word that is initially interpreted as the wrong part of speech or as a different meaning from the one that was intended: *I smell the bacon and waffle between getting up or staying in bed.*

A similar effect occurs when two proper nouns "crash," or appear next to each other with nothing separating them, so that they look like a single unit: *It was too late to try to FaceTime Duncan. I hoped to God Shawna would be there.*

Naughty words and dirty talk

Profanity and sexual terms and situations abound in fiction, especially in genres such as military thrillers, crime and mystery novels, and romance and erotica. And since most style manuals are generally geared toward nonfiction, where such language is rare, advice on how to handle it is scattered. Let's discuss some of the basics.

SPELLING

Always add profanity and sexual terms to the style sheet. Spelling and usage varies, and not all such terms can be found in a standard dictionary. So make your style sheet the dictionary of choice.

When you need a source to cite for your choices, the BuzzFeed Style Guide and the Google Books Ngram Viewer are excellent online resources; Urban Dictionary is crowdsourced (think Wikipedia for filthy minds), so I would count it as slightly less authoritative, though useful for the latest slang. Kia Thomas's compact *A Very Sweary Dictionary*, available in print or ebook form, contains excellent general guidance as well as a word list.

It's often helpful to treat similar terms similarly, especially if you can't find a reference for some of them, for consistency. For example, several common -*ass* words are in *MW11*; *badass* is closed up, and *smart-ass* and *kick-ass* are hyphenated. But what do you do with *dumbass*? It's closed up in *MW11*, with the hyphenated version as an alternate form. The closed version sort of fails the ILF (it looks funny) test, so maybe it needs a hyphen: *dumb-ass*. This is also parallel with "intensifier" -*ass* compounds such as *big-ass, lazy-ass*, and *fancy-ass*, where the hyphen is extremely important (a *big ass photo* is very different from a *big-ass photo*). So for consistency you might hyphenate *bad-ass* and *smart-ass* too, contrary to *MW11*, especially if the author has already done so. Or you could close them up as nouns and hyphenate them as adjectives. When you are dealing with slang, there's a fair amount of wiggle room.

USAGE

Opinions abound about how much profanity is too much, or whether to dial it back by using euphemisms such as *freaking*. The level of profanity will have been well established before the copyediting stage, so you can generally follow the author's lead. But watch for situations where one would expect a character to use the vulgarity, but they don't. A hardboiled black-ops assassin is unlikely to say *effing* or *flippin'* as an intensifier when he really means *fucking*.

Bad people use bad words and say awful things; it's part of their characterization. And characters that the reader is supposed to admire lose their cool, playfully insult their friends, or give someone a well-deserved verbal beatdown. However, watch out for terms such as racial or ableist slurs that may upset readers no matter who is saying them. Depending on context, you can query the author to gently remind them that readers may be offended and ask them to consider finding a way to write around it to convey the nastiness without spelling it out. (See also the section titled "Conscious language" later in this chapter.)

Conversely, watch out for inadvertent innuendo that introduces high hilarity that the author probably didn't intend: *"Look, Mommy, I taught Bingo to turn tricks!"* A good copyeditor has a dirty mind; keep yourself up-to-date on sexual and vulgar slang so you can spot it where it doesn't belong. Channel your inner twelve-year-old and save your author from potential embarrassment.

ACTION

Sex scenes need copyediting too. In addition to having appropriate spelling, grammar, and punctuation, the action should make sense. After all, much of the enjoyment of reading a sex scene is imagining what's happening, and if it's impossible or unintentionally ridiculous, that's pretty much a mood-killer.

So . . . er, picture the action. Do bodies move that way? Is anyone removing the same garment twice? (Or have they not removed it, but suddenly they're naked?) Are there extra body parts? These are all situations you may encounter (and need to query) while copyediting romance and erotica.

THE COPYEDITOR'S COMFORT LEVEL

Does the idea of copyediting fiction of an "adult" nature bother you or make you uncomfortable? That's perfectly all right. It's okay to decline to copyedit genres or themes that disturb you: erotica, child or animal abuse, gore and violence, stories that conflict with your religious beliefs. You can't do a project justice if the subject upsets you. It's perfectly fine to let your clients know what topics you will and won't edit. To each copyeditor their own.

Conscious language

In recent years, the editing world has taken a fresh look at eliminating bias in language: sexism, racism, ageism, ableism, and more. Readers across society, not just those who belong to a marginalized group, may be offended by such language. Yet sometimes words and people, intentionally or not, are biased, unkind, or downright harmful, which fiction, as a representation of life, might seek to reflect. What is a copyeditor who encounters such language in a work of fiction to do?

In an ideal world, a client will have evaluated a manuscript for potentially problematic language and, if necessary, engaged one or more expert reviewers to help identify and resolve any issues before the copyediting stage. Such reviews might involve an expert in conscious language (who looks for biased and outdated language and inappropriate framing in general, in all areas of representation: disability, race, gender identity and expression, sexual orientation, religion, and so on) and/or an authenticity reader (who comments on the manuscript based on specialized knowledge about the subject matter or their own lived experience as a member of one or more communities that are represented in the text). The client would then communicate any relevant decisions and guidelines to the copyeditor. However, these steps don't always happen, and in any case, the copyeditor's focus should be on the language itself rather than absolute accuracy in representation, which is beyond the scope of work at this stage. Still, an attentive copyeditor can save the author and/ or publisher from potentially offending and alienating readers and perpetuating inauthentic or noninclusive language that is no longer tolerated.

During your first "light" pass through the manuscript, watch for the issues discussed later in this section. If you discover potentially problematic language or representation, bring it to your client's attention. If you are working with an indie author, you can discuss it with them directly, whether as a conversation outside the manuscript (by phone or email) or as queries on individual points, depending on the terms of your agreement with the author and how extensive the issues are. If you are working for a publisher, however, you'll need to consider your approach based on the nature of the problem. A single instance of a problematic word choice or usage, such as *sitting Indian style* or *grammar Nazi*, can usually be addressed as a simple query in the manuscript, explaining why the author might want to choose a different term. For larger issues, such as a scene that may misrepresent a real culture's religious rituals or a character's habitual use of racial slurs, it's better to consult your project manager directly; the project manager may be unaware of the conscious language problem and may want to check with the author or higher-level managers before you proceed, or the choice of offensive language may have been discussed and approved at an earlier stage.

Organizations such as editors' associations, corporations, and publishers have started developing guidelines on conscious language for editors to use as reference. If your publisher client provides such a guide, great! They're already on board. Review it and follow it. Guides published by editors' associations and others are available to anyone. But in all cases, I highly recommend that copyeditors communicate with their client about any conscious language issues that they discover in a manuscript and the importance of addressing them. If you are unsure about whether to bring something up, bring it up; it's better to err on the side of querying more assertively than to leave a potentially problematic situation unquestioned. (You are likely not the only person who will notice the problem.) Copyeditors should also continuously keep up-to-date on discussions of conscious language and authenticity, which are evolving rapidly; this section covers only a fraction of the subject. See the Recommended Resources for some places to get started.

Now let's look at some specific points of conscious language to learn about and watch for in the manuscripts we edit.

CHARACTERIZATION

The way a character talks (whether in first-person narration or in dialogue) shows the reader who they are, what their mood is, what their background is, and so on. Some characters are meant to be likeable, while others are evil, and their choice of vocabulary should reflect that. So we don't want the hero of a romance novel, who by definition is supposed to be a lovable character, throwing around casual slurs that might alienate the reader. Conversely, it's possible to convey that a bad actor is a bigot without peppering their speech with racist, homophobic, or transphobic language. How much is too much? Let the genre and overall tone be your guide. Put yourself in the shoes of a reader who might be harmed by the use of such language. Does it serve the story? Who is speaking to whom? Is the language being spoken appropriately for the context? Is the intent to be shocking or offensive, or can the language be toned down and still convey the proper intent without alienating the reader? Depending on context, this may be a query-only situation, or if the client is a publisher, you may wish to ask the project manager for guidance on how to proceed.

SETTING

Language paints a picture and illustrates the setting (time or place) as well as characterization. Many words and phrases that were in common use in past eras have fallen out of favor or been abandoned entirely because they are inaccurate, offensive, or harmful; however, they may be used to convey a particular attitude appropriate to that era.

But should historical accuracy outweigh potential harm to readers? It may not be necessary to use biased language to convey a sense of time or place. Consider the context and ask yourself again: Does it serve the story? Is it necessary? Might it be harmful or alienating to readers? As with all conscious language concerns, if you are working for a publisher, discuss any concerns with your project manager rather than addressing the author directly; they will be aware of previous discussions that have taken place and can advise you whether to let it go or perhaps write up your concerns in a separate note for the publisher to review.

Historical considerations go both ways. For example, the *firemen* on the *Titanic* and other ships of the time were not *firefighters*; they were definitely all men, and their job was to stoke the fires that powered the ship, so changing that term would introduce an error. Similarly, watch out for terms that, although they are more inclusive, do not fit the setting. For example, the word *gay*, as used by homosexual people to describe themselves, dates roughly to the mid-twentieth century; it would be out of place used in this sense in a novel set in the 1600s. When in doubt, check the etymology and history of the term, and query carefully.

OTHER ISSUES REGARDING CONSCIOUS LANGUAGE IN FICTION

Many gendered terms have been replaced in common parlance with their gender-neutral counterparts (*server* instead of *waiter/waitress*; *crewed* instead of *manned*). And an increasing number of novels include characters of all genders and sexual orientations, who use a variety of pronouns, presented in an entirely inclusive manner. All of this is wonderful. Our job as copyeditors is to support this. We can query outdated gendered terms and ensure that LGBTQIA+ characters are handled with respect and equality. But fiction also represents life; a female character might reasonably lament, "I don't want to be a waitress for the rest of my life!" (There's no reason to change *wait-*

ress to *server* here.) Consider context and be careful not to strip the life out of the story.

Watch out for "othering" language. Chapter 4 discussed avoiding words like *exotic* to describe a person's appearance. Similarly, alert the author or publisher to language that assumes whiteness, heterosexuality, cisgender, or other "majority" traits as the default unless there's a good reason for it within the story: if characters' skin color is mentioned only if they are not white, if the teacher tells students to have their mothers pack them a healthy lunch, if a character "looks like a typical guy." It's more inclusive to mention all characters' skin color; to ask students to bring a healthy lunch; to describe the character's build, clothing, and whatever else creates their particular appearance.

Pay attention to words that describe or scenes that depict cultural, religious, or spiritual activities or ceremonies of a real community. They should be accurate and respectful. If the activity appears to be made up or casts the community in a negative light, this could deeply offend members of that group. A gentle query to the author or publisher may be needed.

Keep up-to-date on the meanings of idioms; many have racist or otherwise biased origins. Some are obvious, such as *gypped* and *Dutch treat*; others require some historical knowledge, such as *grandfathered in* and *cakewalk*. You can write a tactful query to suggest appropriate substitutions.

Another common problem is "victim" language used to describe people with disabilities. A person is not *wheelchair bound* or *confined to a wheelchair*; they *use a wheelchair*. Better yet is to simply let the chair exist in the story like any other prop: *He wheeled himself down the ramp.* Unless suffering is the point being made, a person *has asthma*; they don't *suffer from asthma*. A person *has AIDS*; they are not an *AIDS victim*.

Finally, as discussed throughout this section, always be polite and professional in queries, especially when addressing an issue that's outside your personal experience. Keep the tone of your queries dispassionate and nonjudgmental. Do not accuse the author of intending to be offensive or being ignorant of the meaning or history of the language used. Focus on showing why different language might be more inclusive, accurate, unbiased, and so on, and suggest alternatives if you can. Consider providing a citation or link to a book, article, or blog post that explains the issue at hand (such as those listed in the Recommended Resources), and see chapter 2 for general techniques for writing tactful, deferential, helpful queries.

American vs. British vs. Canadian style

Occasionally you may find yourself copyediting a novel by an author from the other side of "the pond" or the other side of the US-Canada border (or a different country altogether, such as India or Australia). It may have been edited in the author's home country, such as England, and now it is being published in the United States. Or you may be working with Canadian English, which has characteristics of both UK and US style as well as its own vocabulary and pronunciation. (See the sidebar titled "Style Guides and Dictionaries for Australian, British, and Canadian English" in chapter 2, as well as the Recommended Resources, for references that can guide you as you copyedit those forms of English.)

To keep things simple in this section, we consider just one example of "translating" one form of English to another: UK to US English. Usually a US copyedit of a UK novel involves "Americanizing" the style to some extent. Let's look at the possibilities.

PUNCTUATION

Most US publishers apply US punctuation style (which also tends to be followed in Canada) to a work that was previously published in the UK. Here are some common examples:

- Change single quotation marks (UK) to double (US) (and vice versa).
- Move commas and periods from outside quotation marks (UK) to inside (US).
- Insert the serial comma (US; UK style tends to omit it).
- Insert periods after titles such as *Mr.*, *Mrs.*, *Ms.*, and *Dr.* (US; omitted in UK style).
- Change *no-one* (UK) to *no one* (US).
- Convert spaced en dashes to closed-up em dashes.

Most of this can be accomplished by cleanup routines such as macros and a careful search-and-replace; it is usually done untracked to avoid creating a messy manuscript. Many publishers do this cleanup before sending the manuscript for copyediting. However, it's not a foolproof process and some manual tweaking is usually needed.

SPELLING

US publishers also usually apply US spelling conventions; however, occasionally UK spelling is retained, particularly if the setting and characters are mostly or all British. Use a good UK dictionary such as the *Oxford English Dictionary* or the *Collins English Dictionary* (both have online versions) to check spellings; the PerfectIt consistency checker can also help.

VOCABULARY AND USAGE

"America and England are separated by a common language." Vocabulary and usage, like spelling, differ on each side of the Atlantic. US publishers choose a certain level of Americanization, depending on the story and its characters and setting; the most common choice is to stet UK terminology unless it is likely to confuse American readers or is unclear in context. Most Americans know that a *lift* is an elevator, a *torch* is a flashlight, a *lorry* is a truck, and so on. But many terms mean different things in US vs. UK English. Consider the following UK terms and their US equivalents: *garden* (yard), *pavement* (sidewalk), *jam* (jelly), and *jelly* (a gelatin dessert). In business-speak, to *table* something means to put it on the agenda for discussion in the UK, whereas in the US it means to postpone discussion indefinitely. *Fanny* (vagina), *knickers* (women's underpants), and *knock up* (impregnate) can cause ribald high hilarity. And there is the US/UK difference between *ground floor* and *first floor*, discussed in chapter 5. US and UK usage also differ in preferred verb forms, articles, and prepositions—for example, *spoiled* vs. *spoilt* and *gotten* vs. *got*; *in the hospital* vs. *in hospital*; *different from/than* vs. *different to*; and *on the weekend* vs. *at the weekend*.

When you come across these differences, consider: Is it in dialogue or first-person narration by a UK speaker? (If so, leave it alone.) Is it clear in context? Will most US readers be able to figure out the meaning? What has the client requested? Avoid making intrusive edits, especially if they border on overexplaining for the reader; query when in doubt.

In addition to consulting reference books, you can familiarize yourself with various dialects of English by reading books and watching films and TV shows that include them. Making friends from around the world on social media (especially if they are also copyeditors) is a wonderful way to expand your vocabulary and knowledge of idioms. Pay attention to how they write and talk. Politely ask the meaning of unfamiliar terms. (And return the favor when they need help understanding your version of English!)

DIALOGUE

No matter what style is being used in narration, characters and first-person narrators must be allowed to speak in their own natural dialect. If a British author is writing American characters, check whether they speak like Americans, and vice versa. Also, dialects vary among natives of any country or region. A Scottish character will not speak like a Londoner, and neither will a person from Yorkshire. (Unless the point is made that they have deliberately changed their speech patterns!) Tread carefully when copyediting dialogue in a dialect with which you are not familiar, and when in doubt, query rather than making outright changes.

8

Copyediting Dialogue

Dialogue (which for our purposes includes first-person narration) constitutes a large part of fiction and can be a challenge to edit. The most important consideration is to keep a light hand and edit only as much as is necessary for clarity while allowing characters to retain their voice.

Why is dialogue special?

Some publishers instruct their copyeditors not to edit dialogue at all; only queries are allowed. I suspect that this directive is the result of too many prescriptive copyeditors trying to shoehorn dialogue into some standard of grammatical perfection. After all, dialogue is the unique expression of each character, and people don't normally "edit" themselves in casual speech. We speak in fragments, we backtrack, we use the wrong word, we hem and haw, we use informal grammar. And although dialogue generally should be edited with a light hand, its presentation still needs to serve the reader and the story. A skilled copyeditor preserves the voices expressed in dialogue while ensuring that the way they are represented is not an obstruction for the reader.

Let's look at some ways that dialogue adds to the flavor of a work of fiction.

AUTHOR VOICE

A fiction author is creating a world and its characters, telling a story, setting a mood. Nonfiction conveys information, and sometimes fiction does too, but that's not its primary motivation. And the words that an author puts in their characters' mouths helps mold those characters into what the author needs to tell that story.

CHARACTER VOICE

Remember the iconic opening line of *Huckleberry Finn*? "You don't know about me without you have read a book by the name of *The Adventures of Tom Sawyer*; but that ain't no matter." We've already learned a lot about Huck from that single sentence. "Correcting" it to "You don't know about me unless you have read a book called *The Adventures of Tom Sawyer*, but that doesn't matter" would remove all of that flavor and characterization. And the author would very rightly want to clobber the copyeditor over the head for doing so.

Characters need to speak in accordance with their background. They have accents, they have a certain education level (or none at all), they use regional slang and professional jargon, they speak in languages in which they aren't fluent, and so on. They speak in dialects, each of which has its own idiosyncratic vocabulary and grammar (*She got a drink from the bubbler*; *The dishes need washed*).

If dialogue isn't authentic, it pulls readers out of the story. The author may have it right; if it's outside your experience, don't edit it to be wrong. Conversely, if the author is writing outside their experience, they may need some help getting it right (for example, to avoid having Native characters speaking in one-syllable words and grunts or Black characters speaking only "jive"). So especially in dialogue, think twice before making that change. Check resources such as the *Dictionary of American Regional English*, or go online and ask people (particularly fellow editors) who are familiar with that dialect or language. (See also the section titled "Conscious language" in chapter 7.)

"THAT'S HOW PEOPLE TALK"

People stutter, they speak in incomplete sentences, they interrupt each other, they mispronounce things, they're speaking a second language in muddled syntax, they use slang, they use flat adverbs (*Come quick!*), they use *lay* and *lie* interchangeably, they have verbal habits (and sometimes those are the author's verbal habits). Inexperienced copyeditors (and especially those new to copyediting fiction) often want to "fix" a line of dialogue because it's not "perfect." And often the correct answer is to leave it, because the meaning is clear and *that's how people talk*.

Copyediting fiction is not for prescriptivists. And I say this as a recovering prescriptivist. But it's especially true for dialogue. Even though it's in print on the page, natural human speech is extemporaneous. It hasn't been edited to death. You can't stuff a novel into perfect *CMOS* style. You can't stuff a novel into any of the "rules" I've given here because each one is different. Yes, there may be a house style to apply, but let the characters have their voice, and check your prescriptivism at the door.

This principle also applies to first-person narration, which is just a form of dialogue with the reader—especially when the narrator addresses the reader directly (*Do you know what I mean?*). In first person, the narrator is talking in their own voice.

However, the copyeditor must also serve the reader. The presentation of the dialogue should not make the reader stumble or stop to figure out what the character or narrator is saying and pull them out of the story, whether it's opaque spelling, or awkward punctuation, or anachronistic language, or inauthentic or overwritten dialect.

CMOS has some guidance, but it was designed for nonfiction. And fiction authors often make different and deliberate stylistic choices that don't appear in any style guide. This is one of the places where the manuscript often becomes its own style resource.

Now that we've talked about the basic philosophy of copyediting dialogue, let's get into the mechanics.

Dialogue tags and action beats

Dialogue tags and action beats are a point of confusion for many writers and editors. In this section we'll go over the differences, how to punctuate them, and why they are not interchangeable. Let's start with some simple definitions and examples:

A *dialogue tag* tells what was said and who said it, and perhaps how. The dialogue and the dialogue tag together form a complete sentence:

"It'll be okay," he said.

In this example, *he said* is the dialogue tag. The dialogue ends with a comma, and *he said* (lowercase *h*) completes the sentence.

An *action beat* is a narrative description of action that identifies the speaker but does not describe the dialogue. The action beat is a separate sentence from the dialogue:

"It'll be okay." He stood up.

In this example, *He stood up* is the action beat. The dialogue ends with a period because it stands alone. *He* (capital *H*) is the speaker; *He stood up* is a complete sentence that does not convey how *he* spoke.

Now let's look at more variations and distinguishing features of dialogue tags and action beats.

DIALOGUE TAG VARIATIONS

Here's our basic dialogue tag example again:

"It'll be okay," he said.

A dialogue tag can also go before the dialogue:

He said, "It'll be okay."

It can go after the dialogue, but inverted. This creates a slightly elegant variation. It's not incorrect, but depending on the context, it can sometimes be overdone. Using a pronoun instead of a name gives a slightly more archaic, poetic feel.

"It'll be okay," said Kyle.

"Forsooth, a rider approacheth," said she.

The dialogue might end with a question mark or an exclamation point (note that a comma is not needed):

"What are you doing tomorrow?" Juana said.

"I'm so happy for you!" Taz said.

So far, our examples all use the verb *said*. However, sometimes a stronger or more descriptive verb is needed:

"Here he comes!" Enzo shouted excitedly.

They told the boy, "Today is my birthday."

However, not all verbs are appropriate for dialogue tags. Let's discuss that next.

VERBS OF UTTERANCE

A *verb of utterance* describes the act of speaking. *Said* is the classic verb of utterance. It's straightforward. The reader doesn't really see the word *said*. It doesn't draw attention to itself; it simply explains who said what. It disappears. There's nothing wrong with good old *said*. Yes, even with questions:

She said, "Do you really have no idea?"

Asked is also a perfectly cromulent verb of utterance—*said*'s invisible counterpart for questions:

"What do you want to do about dinner?" he asked.

However, when we move beyond *said* and *asked*, only certain verbs can reasonably describe the act of speech—and some are more reasonable than others. Let's look at some examples:

RIGHT: she screamed, he muttered, I wheezed
WRONG: I grimaced, she shuddered, he fudged

You can *groan, breathe, whisper,* and even (metaphorically) *spit* words. You can't *shrug, smile, anticipate,* or *cringe* them. A verb of utterance has to describe something you do to create words and sentences.

There are shades of appropriateness, however. *Shouted*, sure. *Sputtered, agreed, begged*, okay. *Chuckled*, maybe (if it's short). And then there are *ground out, gritted out*, and *bit out*, usually attributed to angry male characters; these verbs obviously aren't literal when applied to speaking, but they're established as idiom and are prevalent in fiction, so they generally can be left in, unless they're overused. Occasionally authors attempt to use words like *stomped* and *bristled* as verbs of utterance. Just no. (Unless the publisher or author has decreed that any word may be used as a verb of utterance—which occasionally happens—in which case you just let it go and repeat: "It's not my book.")

Use and acceptance of "creative" verbs of utterance varies widely among authors, publishers, and editors. You may be told that only *said* and *asked* are acceptable, and others must be changed or queried. Other manuscripts have more leeway. For the former, you'll need to scrutinize verbs of utterance more closely. For the latter, borderline verbs such as *encouraged* or *accused* may be acceptable. But if the text starts to read like no two dialogue tags are the same, you may need to query and ask the author to consider changing some back to the invisible *said*.

When you are determining whether a verb of utterance that follows dialogue works, try putting it before the dialogue:

"I won't do it!" she defied.

She defied, "I won't do it!"

Putting the verb next to the dialogue often helps show why it doesn't work. In this case, the tag could be changed to *she said* or *she said defiantly*, or (with an accompanying query to the author) turned into an action beat:

"I won't do it!" She crossed her arms defiantly.

Also, consider the context and the length of what is being said:

"Oh, Heathcliff," she sighed.

"[Five sentences]," she sighed.

It's pretty hard to *sigh* or *grunt* or *hiss* a whole paragraph! Ask yourself: Is it physically possible? Is the sense of the verb conveyed by the speech itself? If a change is needed, make a suggestion or two. Explain to the author why the verb might trip readers up, or why they might find it awkward or comical.

FIXING INCORRECT DIALOGUE TAGS AND ACTION BEATS

The correct structure of dialogue tags and action beats is one of the biggest sources of confusion in fiction. It's also one of the few areas where you have to follow the rules! Let's look at some examples of common errors and how to fix them.

> WRONG: "I hadn't heard about that," he frowned. This is a dialogue tag with an incorrect verb of utterance (you can't frown words).
>
> WRONG: "I hadn't heard about that," and he frowned. Call this a comma splice, call it a run-on sentence, either way it's wrong.

Either of these can be fixed as follows:

> RIGHT: "I hadn't heard about that." He frowned. The dialogue tag has been turned into an action beat. He spoke the words, and he frowned: two separate actions, two separate sentences.
>
> RIGHT: "I hadn't heard about that," he said, frowning. The incorrect verb of utterance has been changed to the traditional *said*, and *frowned* has been turned into the gerund *frowning*, describing the person's expression as he spoke.

What if the sentence is turned around?

> WRONG: Rita looked up, "Flowers? For me?" *Looked up* is not a verb of utterance.
>
> RIGHT: Rita looked up and exclaimed, "Flowers? For me?" A proper verb of utterance has been inserted (with a query to confirm the word choice).
>
> RIGHT: Rita looked up. "Flowers? For me?" The comma has been changed to a period to create an action beat, and context makes it clear who is speaking, so no tag is needed.

Here's another common error:

> WRONG: "I'm not kidding." She said. This dialogue tag is not formatted correctly.
>
> RIGHT: "I'm not kidding," she said. Change the period to a comma and lowercase *she*, and all is well.

The following examples show the correct formatting only:

Dialogue tag interrupting dialogue (same sentence): "I don't know about you," she said, "but I'm staying here." The sentence continues after the dialogue tag, so the tag is preceded and followed by a comma, and the sentence continues with a lowercase letter.

Dialogue tag interrupting dialogue (new sentence): "I'm leaving," he said. "You can come with me if you want." A new sentence begins after the dialogue tag, so the tag is preceded by a comma and followed by a period, and the new sentence begins with a capital letter.

Action beat interrupting dialogue (same sentence): "I could tell you"—I pinned him with my steely gaze—"but then I'd have to kill you." Many writers and editors are unsure how to handle this construction. And the answer is *Just like this*. Most US publishers request this format. The dialogue is continuous and is not actually interrupted by the action, so the em dashes go outside the quotation marks. Ensure that the second opening quote mark (before *but*) is turned the right way; Word likes to turn it the other way following a dash. A separate search for a dash followed by a closing quote mark (—") is a good idea; check search results one at a time so you don't change those that are correct (such as "But—").

Action beat interrupting dialogue (new sentence): "Well, I guess that's all—" She looked around. "Wait, where's the baby?" If the dialogue itself is interrupted, the break is indicated by an em dash inside the quotation marks, the action beat becomes a complete sentence, and the new sentence of dialogue begins with a capital letter.

COMBINING DIALOGUE TAGS WITH ACTION

The following is a common and tricky combination of a dialogue tag and an action:

"I don't understand," Phyllis said, and looked away.

Writers, editors, and publishers disagree about whether to use that comma after *said*. Although this type of sentence is not technically parallel, it's perfectly understandable with or without the comma. Ultimately, it's a simple style choice, either the author's or publisher's, or yours if no preference is given. (I prefer to use it, to separate the tag from the action.) However, another option is to insert a pronoun, turning the sentence into two independent clauses:

"I don't understand," Phyllis said, and she looked away.

DOUBLE DIALOGUE TAGS

Be on the lookout for double dialogue tags, which occur when two tags are attached to the same piece of dialogue:

"Well, let's see. I got up and went to school as usual," I said, "and I felt fine until just after lunchtime. But around one o'clock I started to feel a little dizzy," I said.

This is easily fixed by removing one of the tags (it's usually best to keep the first one, to quickly show readers who is speaking) and adjusting the punctuation as needed.

WHEN "DIALOGUE" ISN'T DIALOGUE

Want to be a rock star? Learn to recognize "dialogue" that isn't dialogue. Sometimes what looks like dialogue is not actually dialogue but simply the object of a verb:

WRONG: the equivalent of shouting, "Fire!" in a crowded theater
RIGHT: the equivalent of shouting "Fire!" in a crowded theater

In this example, *"Fire!"* isn't actually being shouted; it's simply being discussed, and it's the object of the verb *shouting*. So no dialogue tag exists here, and thus no comma.

WRONG: I longed to hear her say, *I love you.*
RIGHT: I longed to hear her say *I love you.*

WRONG: He would say weird things like, "Give me your eyebrows," as if they were completely normal.
RIGHT: He would say weird things like "Give me your eyebrows" as if they were completely normal.

WRONG: Her body language screamed, "Don't talk to me," as she shivered in the dim light.

RIGHT: Her body language screamed "Don't talk to me" as she shivered in the dim light.

None of these are dialogue; they are not things that are being spoken, but things that are being spoken *of*, described, or reported.

This construction also holds for signs, quoted speech, and other reported words:

WRONG: The sign said, DO NOT ENTER.
RIGHT: The sign said DO NOT ENTER.

WRONG: How could he say, "I'm sorry," when he clearly wasn't?
RIGHT: How could he say "I'm sorry" when he clearly wasn't?

WRONG: She frantically scribbled, "Back in 5 minutes," on the notepad.
RIGHT: She frantically scribbled "Back in 5 minutes" on the notepad.

WRONG: A weak, "I'm over here," was all I could manage.
RIGHT: A weak "I'm over here" was all I could manage.

HE SAID, SHE SAID . . .

Watch for overuse or underuse of dialogue tags and action beats in long exchanges. Context matters.

Too many dialogue tags or action beats in a row can be intrusive, especially for short utterances or only two speakers:

Anuk said, "We're nearly out of water."
"What?" Lumi said.
"The skin is almost dry," Anuk said.
Lumi said, "But we have at last four days' travel remaining."

This is less true when multiple people are speaking, but even then it can be overdone.

Depending on context, the distraction can be reduced by deleting a few tags or beats or by changing a few tags into beats (or vice versa):

Anuk said, "We're nearly out of water."
"What?"

"The skin is almost dry."

"But we have at last four days' travel remaining." Lumi looked defeated.

If you are only deleting a few simple tags, a query explaining the edits should be sufficient. If more extensive revision is needed, you can either simply describe the problem and ask the author to revise accordingly, or offer a few edits and explain that they are suggestions or examples.

Conversely, long exchanges with few or no dialogue tags or action beats can leave the copyeditor (and by extension, the reader) wondering who's talking, especially if there are three or more speakers or the content of the dialogue doesn't provide context clues. Usually there should be a tag or beat every three or four lines (however, pacing may dictate that there be more or fewer). Solutions for this problem are similar to those for having too many tags or beats:

- Add a few tags or beats to clarify who's speaking (and query the author for confirmation).
- If you're truly lost (or think that readers might be), query the author, explaining the problem and asking them to add some tags or beats, or perhaps revise the dialogue slightly, to eliminate confusion.

PARAGRAPHING

We all learned the "rule" about a new paragraph for each new speaker, but occasionally for rhythm or pacing, an author breaks this rule. It can be effective if not overdone—for example, if characters are talking over each other in quick succession. If you encounter this format, query the author or publisher before attempting to break the dialogue into paragraphs.

Continuous, multiparagraph passages of dialogue by a single speaker are uncommon in fiction; such dialogue is usually broken up with dialogue tags, action beats, and interjections from other speakers. But they do exist. Just as in nonfiction, each new paragraph begins with opening quotation marks, and only the last paragraph ends with closing quotation marks.

TOM SWIFTIES

In a Tom Swifty, the dialogue tag is a pun on the content of the dialogue.[1] Tom Swifties can be sneaky, and the inadvertent ones aren't always as obvious as the ones that people construct to be funny, but they turn up now and then. The second example here illustrates a variation on a Tom Swifty that appears more often than you might think: a simple echo between dialogue and tag, most likely the result of an incomplete revision.

"We just struck oil!" Tom gushed.

"Sadly, that's not an option," he said sadly.

In a humorous context, Tom Swifties may be intentional, but even if so, they can sound awkward and the joke may fall flat with readers. It's worth a query to the author to ask if the pun was intentional.

Punctuating dialogue

Punctuation marks are the road signs of dialogue. They delineate who is speaking. They show where sentences start, stop, pause, trail off, and are interrupted. They convey emotion and volume. And they give helpful clues to the reader. For example, many writers and editors feel that semicolons do not belong in fiction, especially in dialogue: they're "too formal" or people don't "speak" semicolons. Semicolons are less common in genres with a more casual register such as romance and cozy mysteries and more common in those that are more formal, such as historical and literary fiction. And although authors may rightfully choose to omit them, semicolons can be a useful signpost for readers when used correctly—even in dialogue.

Let's look at some specific uses of punctuation in dialogue.

---

1. See, for example, "The Joy of Tom Swifties," *Merriam-Webster*, https://www.merriam-webster.com/words-at-play/tom-swifties-puns-that-turn-adverbs-into-punchlines.

INTERRUPTIONS (DASHES)

When dialogue is abruptly cut off, use a dash. Let context be your guide. Picture the scene and imagine how the words are being spoken to determine whether the speech is being interrupted.

"But I—"

"I don't want to hear another word!"

Sometimes an interrupted sentence is broken by an intervening paragraph, either narration or dialogue. Use context to determine whether the continued dialogue should begin with a dash and whether it should be capped or lowercased. For example, a new sentence begins with a capital letter, no dash:

"So then I talked to Christine and—"
"Do you mean Catherine?"
"Yes, sorry, Catherine. And she said we have nothing to worry about."

If an interrupted sentence continues after the interruption, it begins with a dash and a lowercase letter:

"So then I talked to Christine and—"
I jumped as the door slammed open. Lydia gestured for me to continue.
"—and she said we have nothing to worry about."

The interruption may also be an action beat, followed by dialogue from a different speaker:

"So then I talked to Christine and—"
BANG! I jumped as the door slammed open and Trace stormed in.
"What the hell are you doing here?" His rage filled the room.

PAUSES AND TRAILING OFF (ELLIPSES)

Use an ellipsis to indicate a pause or trailing off. Look at the context; sometimes authors use a dash where an ellipsis is a better fit, and vice versa. When in doubt, query the author and ask what their intent is.

"You can't . . . Never mind."

"But can you . . . can you help him?"

"She kicked me in the . . ." He looked down.

Similar guidelines apply for capitalizing the word after the ellipsis. Does it seem to be starting a new sentence? Has the author used a consistent style for such constructions throughout?

Most publishers have a house style of three ellipsis points only for fiction; however, you may occasionally see four-dot ellipses (period plus three ellipsis points after a complete sentence) in things like real or fictional extracts from printed or quoted material.

COMMA AFTER AN ELLIPSIS?

Standard dialogue style calls for a comma preceding a dialogue tag. But what if the dialogue ends in an ellipsis? *CMOS* says to include it; however, the house style of most US publishers omits it. If your client has a preference, follow it.

"Well . . . ," said Eloise. (*CMOS*)

"Well . . ." said Eloise. (*common practice*)

OPENING APOSTROPHES

Just as for quotation marks following dashes, Word likes to mess with opening apostrophes and turn them into open single quotation marks. Follow the same procedure: check them carefully and run searches as necessary.

WRONG: 'cause, 'er, 'im, 'til
RIGHT: 'cause, 'er, 'im, 'til

STUTTERING

Stuttering comes with its own set of rules. These are the most common (see also the discussion of stuttering and hesitation in chapter 3 for other examples):

- Use hyphens between repeated letter sounds.
- Use hyphens, en dashes, or em dashes between repeated words, depending on author or publisher preference, if stated.
- Repeat both letters for combined letter sounds (*Th-th-th-that's all, folks!*).
- Use an initial capped letter only at the beginning of the sentence. Exception: Repeat the capped letter if the word is a proper noun.

"B-b-bu-but I-I'm scared!"

"I-I-I don't know what you mean!"

"Wh-wh-what are you doing?"

"Ch-Charles, come back!"

OH, OH, OH . . .

Sometimes an author or publisher distinguishes between common phrases such as *oh no* or *oh my God* (where you would omit the comma) and phrases that use an introductory or exclamatory *oh* before a name, endearment, or phrase, as in *oh, honey* or *oh, I don't know* (where you would include the comma). Sometimes they want the comma no matter what, common phrase or not.

If a style is given, follow it. If not, follow the prevailing style if one exists. If the author seems to be letting pacing and emotion dictate the use of commas in these phrases, it's fine to leave them. And it doesn't hurt to run a final search pass for *oh* to review all instances.

Note that there is never a comma with the vocative *O* (*O Lord, hear our prayer*).

Here are some common examples of *oh* phrases that may or may not include the comma in each manuscript:

oh yes; oh no
oh, my; oh my goodness
oh, please!
oh God; oh my God; omigod

A word about *God*: Although *CMOS* prescribes always capping the name of the Abrahamic God, in fiction it is often lowercased when used in expressions such as *oh my god*, especially in YA fiction. Follow the author's lead unless the publisher insists on capping *God*.

ADDING EMPHASIS

The treatment of emphasized words doesn't generally involve punctuation, but let's talk about it quickly here. Occasionally you may encounter a sentence where the emphasis could be on multiple words, but the author hasn't indicated where the natural emphasis would be for context. You can help readers get it right in their head by adding italics to show where the speaker is punching a word or words (with a query asking for confirmation). For example:

> "How did he find out?"
> "*I* didn't say anything!" (Someone else did!)

> "I told you not to say anything to him."
> "I *didn't* say anything!" (Because you told me not to!)

> "Did you actually say that to him?"
> "I didn't *say* anything!" (But my face gave it away!)

> "What did you say to him?"
> "I didn't say *anything*!" (Not even one word!)

SPOKEN PUNCTUATION

Occasionally characters speak punctuation (and these constructions can also appear in narration). The punctuation that they are speaking should be spelled out to show that it is being said.

> "This is my den-slash-junk-room."

> "I don't care whether your quote-unquote boyfriend is a hobo or a billionaire!"

Numbers in dialogue

Traditionally, numbers in dialogue are spelled out, to convey exactly how they were said. On the other hand, some numbers are difficult to parse if we spell them out, and a lot of spelled-out numbers in quick succession becomes tiresome to read. Generally, simple generic numbers can be spelled out:

"That jerk owes me a hundred bucks!"

"Back in the nineties I was quite the ladies' man."

"I got home on the twenty-sixth."

But let's not get carried away. For example, precise dollar amounts, years, and numbers with a specific meaning are usually best rendered in digits:

"Your total comes to $397.64."

"My mother lived from 1942 to 2004."

"But after 9/11, everything changed."

If you spell out a number, consider how it is being pronounced. How do you pronounce *$1,500*? "Fifteen hundred dollars"? "One thousand five hundred dollars"? How about *$100*? "A hundred" or "one hundred"? Maybe "a hunnert" in the speaker's dialect. And is it "dollars" or "bucks"?

The following is a partial list of suggestions for dealing with various types of numbers in dialogue. These are not rigid style rules; they are, however, the treatment most often encountered in traditionally published fiction.

Spell out:

- round numbers (including ordinals) (two thousand years, the five hundredth time)
- ages (twenty-two years old)
- heights (six one, five foot three)
- simple times (two o'clock, eleven forty-five, fifteen seconds)

Use digits:

- years (1885)
- numbers with decimals (14.2 parsecs)
- brand names (WD-40)
- numbers on displays (3800 RPM)
- specific times (such as digital clocks) (12:04)
- gun calibers (.22)
- course numbers (Calculus 201)

- phone numbers (555-5555)
- highway numbers (Highway 67)
- Bible chapter/verse (Job 19:23–24)
- thickly clustered numbers

Sounds and nonverbal dialogue

Grunts and noises generally aren't in the dictionary, so sometimes we need to create our own ways to represent them. Does the spelling convey the correct sound and meaning? Does the punctuation make sense? Check to see if the expression is in your dictionary. A previous style sheet may give you specific or general guidance on how to handle repeated letters or spelling for nonverbal utterances (for example, how many *m*'s in *umm?*).

Here are some common examples of nonverbal dialogue:

- *uh-huh* (yes), *uh-uh* (no), *nuh-uh* (teenage no)
- *mmm-hmm, aarrgh, ummm, shh* (Which letters are repeated? How many times?)
- Is it *oohs and aahs* or *oohs and ahhs*? (Both are common. Also, note that *oooh* and *ohhh* are different sounds.)

Unspoken dialogue

Dialogue is not always spoken aloud. It can be thought (directly or indirectly), imagined, mouthed, remembered, sent telepathically, and so on. See Beth Hill's *The Magic of Fiction* and Louise Harnby's *Editing Fiction at Sentence Level* for excellent discussions about formats for unspoken dialogue in different narrative tenses and points of view.

A previous style sheet may guide you on how to treat these elements. In the absence of one, and if the manuscript is inconsistent, you have some decisions to make. See the section on dialogue in chapter 3 for suggestions. Here's a review of the most common types:

- Spoken: "I wonder if he still loves me."
- Direct thought: *I wonder if he still loves me.*
- Indirect thought: I wondered if he still loved me.
- Imagined dialogue: What could I say to him? *Do you still love me?*

- Mouthed dialogue: I cried out, "Do you still love me?" He mouthed, *Of course I do.*
- Remembered dialogue: His words came back to me: *Of course I still love you.*
- Telepathic dialogue: *I love you,* he replied. (Occasionally telepathic communication is rendered in roman with quotation marks, with context cues indicating the telepathy, or italic with quotation marks.)

When copyediting direct thought, watch for the sometimes unnecessary tag *he thought*—or worse, *he thought to himself.* (Unless it's telepathy, who else would he be thinking to?) Context should make it clear that his thoughts are inside his own head. These can usually be safely deleted, with a query to the author to explain the reason.

Also pay close attention in first-person past-tense narration when the narrator slips into present-tense direct thought. If the style for direct thought is italic, make sure that such internal thoughts are italic as well:

I shifted uncomfortably in my seat. *What am I doing here?*

If the style for direct thought is roman, make sure that context makes the switch from narration to internal thought clear. If not, a query may be in order.

E-dialogue

In contemporary stories, characters email, tweet, post on Facebook, text each other, and more. Electronic and online communication is usually casual and has its own style and rules (or lack thereof). For example, many people don't write full sentences or use formal punctuation in text messages. Online communication sometimes contains pictographs, either ASCII-style emoticons (¯_(ツ)_/¯ or :^p) or graphics (♥ or 😂). Textspeak also has its own acronyms (TBH, LMK, WTF).

Publishers often designate Word character styles for text messages, computer input, and other electronic expression.

I typed back, See ya later, tater.

In the absence of specific styles, italics are a common choice, with context cues to identify the nature of the message.

Her phone chimed: *Meet you there.*

He tweeted, *BREAKING: @potus has arrived on the scene in Atlanta.*

In long strings of back-and-forth text messages, if context does not show who's texting, other clues may be needed to keep the "speakers" straight: dialogue tags or action beats, different indents, different fonts, or alternating left and right justification for each speaker. See Carol Saller's post about formatting text messages in fiction at the *CMOS Shop Talk* blog for more information. Gretchen McCulloch's *Because Internet* is also a good resource for e-dialogue.

Translations of non-English dialogue

Occasionally non-English dialogue is followed by a translation into English:

"Habibi!" My friend!

He raised a hand in greeting. *"Ik geb denna traga."* I mean you no harm.

Since the translation is essentially an explanatory aside for the benefit of the reader, it goes outside the quotation marks. The original language and the English translation can be styled in a variety of ways. If the author has used a consistent, sensible style, follow it; if not, establish one.

Here are some suggested options:

"Venez avec moi," she said. *Come with me.*

"Venez avec moi," she said. Come with me.

"Venez avec moi." (Come with me.)

Dialect and informal dialogue

Dialogue should represent how each character would talk. However, when dealing with dialect and informal styles of expression, authenticity requires the copyeditor to proceed with caution (and plenty of tactful queries). Here are some guidelines. (See also the section titled "Conscious language" in chapter 7.)

- Characters sometimes have a better grasp of grammar and usage than the author does! Help them out. Errors should be the character's, not the author's. If the character normally speaks in a formal and meticulous manner and the author has chosen a word or a construction that the character wouldn't use (such as *between Rhys and I*), suggest a correction and query.
- Conversely, characters should not speak too formally or correctly if that is not their voice, especially in first-person narration. For example, a narrator with no formal education who can't read and has not spent a lot of time around people with strong language skills is unlikely to use the "big" words in the following examples:

  I thought she sounded noncommittal.

  George's mercurial behavior annoyed him.

  Pay attention to whose head or point of view you're in, and verify that the voice matches the character.
- Be careful about overcorrecting; you may need to *reduce* the formality level to keep a character's voice true (always with a query to the author explaining why, offering suggestions, and seeking confirmation). Check the authenticity of the character's word choice, syntax, and idioms if they speak a certain dialect (for example, *roundabout* vs. *traffic circle* vs. *rotary*). Characters who speak a language that is not their native tongue may have particular speech patterns (for example, Russian speakers who aren't fluent in English often omit articles because Russian doesn't have them: *Where is kitchen?*). Let the character's overall speaking style and characterization guide you as you watch for dialogue that doesn't quite fit, and query anything that is unclear or seems inconsistent.
- Countries and languages are not monoliths; vocabulary, grammar, and accents vary by region. In Wisconsin we drink

from a *bubbler*, or what people from most other regions of the United States call a *water fountain*. If a thirsty character who was born and raised in America's Dairyland asks where to find a water fountain, that's going to ring false to readers who are Wisconsin natives. But if you are not familiar with this regional usage, it would be wrong to change it. Check your prescriptivism before "correcting." Do some research first. Check online sources such as the *Dictionary of American Regional English* or Google Books Ngram Viewer. Ask people (and especially editors) who are from the region in question for guidance. You can also query the author and ask for confirmation.

Conversely, people read. They watch movies. They talk to other people. There is no rule (other than anachronism issues) that says that people are forbidden from ever using phrases outside their own personal time and place.

- Watch for overwriting of accents and dialect; in addition to being difficult to read, they can also devolve into stereotypes and caricatures. Skilled authors provide descriptive hints ("he spoke in a thick Scottish brogue"), vocabulary choices, and a *few* creative spellings to suggest the flavor of the character's speech rather than phonetically spelling every accented word.

Now let's look at some of the mechanics of copyediting dialect and informal dialogue.

DIALECTS AND ACCENTS

Everyone speaks a dialect in some form, and everyone has an accent, whether they realize it or not. Dialects have their own rules; they're not "sloppy" or "nonstandard" English. Dialects and accents should not be overdone; make sure they are authentic, respectful, and contemporary to the story, rather than mocking, offensive, or outdated. When dialects and accents are represented correctly, the spelling and punctuation should convey accurate pronunciation and meaning, and the grammar should be authentic to that dialect.

Apostrophes indicate missing or elided letters and sounds, as well as contractions: *'cause, ag'in, I'mma, doin'*. Record all such variants; also record whether a particular form is used only by a certain character. Check that leading apostrophes on words like *'em* (*them*) and *'er* (*her*) are turned the correct way. And for heaven's sake, put the apostrophe in *y'all* (*you all*) in the right place; it's incorrectly rendered as *ya'll* far too often.

Check the spelling: does it convey the appropriate sense and pronunciation? There's a subtle dialect difference between *yuh* and *ya* (meaning *you*). Is *because* shortened to *cuz, 'cuz,* or *'cause*? Any of these might be a legitimate choice if it serves characterization.

As always, be careful when copyediting a dialect that is unfamiliar to you; beware a foolish consistency, and query if the dialect seems off rather than trying to correct it yourself.

SLANG

Slang terms can have variant spellings, and a standard dictionary may not help you! Try alternatives such as the BuzzFeed Style Guide, Urban Dictionary, and Google Books Ngram Viewer. (See the Recommended Resources for more options.) Occasionally an author has a preference that differs from these sources. Check to see whether the pronunciation and spelling support the meaning. And just as for "dirty words" (see chapter 7), always add slang terms to the style sheet to show which variant is being used.

Here are some frequent fliers (some are in *MW11* and some are not):

damn it/dammit
geez/jeez
God damn it/goddammit
helluva (*hell of a*)
outta (*out of*)
son of a bitch/son-of-a-bitch
whaddya/whadja/whatcha (these could variously represent *what do you/what did you/what are you*)
whoop-de-do
Woot!
young'uns

NICKNAMES

Characters often have nicknames—and different characters may address each other differently. A person may be known to everyone by their nickname. Or perhaps only a particular person uses it. Record these relationships and habits on your style sheet.

Familial names also fall under this category. Is it spelled *Mama*, *Mamma*, or *Momma*? People usually use the same form when addressing family members; it's unusual for a person to call their parent both *Father* and *Papa*. Unless there's a compelling reason for variety, these forms should generally be treated consistently.

Anachronisms

In noncontemporary fiction, keep an ear out for anachronisms in dialogue as well as in narration (see also chapter 9). Was that term in use with that meaning during the character's lifetime? *MW11* has dates of first known use, but they don't always apply to each meaning, especially for variants such as slang or technological terms. You may need to do a bit of hunting. Generally a little bit of leeway is fine; if your dictionary gives a term a date of 1911 and the character is speaking it in 1905, that's probably close enough since a term may have been spoken well before it appeared in print. However, if Lucy in 1905 is using a term that first appeared in 1965, that should raise an eyebrow and perhaps a query.

On the other hand, watch for overly outdated language. Would a teenager in the present day say something is *the bee's knees* or call an old car a *jalopy*? It's possible, but unlikely; there would have to be a good explanation.

However, also bear in mind the overall voice. A story may be set well in the past or in a fantasy world but have a more casual, humorous, or satirical tone that allows for more modern language. Conversely, a fantasy novel may have an archaic feel, so that while modern-sounding language may not be wrong, it would be out of place. Let the overall tone of the piece be your guide for when to research and query as needed.

9

When Fact and Fiction Collide

As Mark Twain famously wrote in *Pudd'nhead Wilson's New Calendar*, "Truth is stranger than fiction, but it is because Fiction is obliged to stick to possibilities; Truth isn't." Twain was right. Readers expect the details of the story to hang together. It can't break its own internal rules unless there's a very good reason. And if it is set in the world as we know it, all of the factual elements must generally ring true. But it can be difficult when revising a story to keep all those little interrelated details from falling apart and disrupting suspension of disbelief. That's where the copyeditor comes in and (hopefully) saves the day.

This holds true for stories that take place in invented worlds as well as those that live in the reality of our own universe. A story's world may have different rules of physics, biology, geography, sociology, magic, and so on, and once established, those rules must be followed consistently. The more different and intricate those rules are, the more detailed both your style sheet and your attention must be.

Let's look at some of the areas where things can go haywire.

Physics bloopers
Our motto for this chapter is this: "Picture the action. Could it happen?" The sun does not shine in a west-facing window in the morning—unless we are in a fictional world where the sun rises in the west, in which case the sun does not shine in an *east*-facing window in the morning. Water cannot freeze solid in five minutes—unless there is an explanation. When

you are standing in a brightly lit room at night, and you look out a closed window into the darkness, you see not whatever is happening outside, but your own reflection—and vice versa for looking into the dark interior of a house from outside on a sunny day.

Ask yourself whether what is being depicted is how things really work (within the world of the story). Put yourself in the scene and interact with it yourself. Think about what it would look like: How does that object move, how does a person operate it, what does it sound like, what would happen if someone did that thing in real life? If it's unlikely or impossible, write a query to let the author know and suggest solutions if you can.

Action bloopers

In chapter 1, I talked about how the copyeditor is like the continuity supervisor on a movie set. Both are responsible for ensuring that people and objects don't suddenly move around, appear or disappear, or change to something else entirely. This is often the result of incomplete revisions in earlier drafts. Here are a few examples:

- *Drop-in characters or objects:* Stefan and Arthur enter an empty room and have a conversation, and suddenly Desirae starts speaking, as if she has been there the whole time. A waiter takes Sakura's order in a restaurant and leaves, and she immediately begins eating food that the waiter hasn't brought yet.
- *Repeated action or speech:* Cesar takes off his shoes twice in the same scene. Duncan tells Ava something that he just told her, and there's no reason for the repetition or for Ava to have forgotten or not heard it, and Ava treats it as new information.
- *Missing action or speech:* Jace removes the wet laundry from the washing machine, then hauls it upstairs, folds it, and puts it away without ever going near the dryer. Aric mentions that Helfrida told him something at a particular time and place, when the plot dictates that she couldn't have.
- *Transformation:* A stallion turns into a gelding. Tea becomes coffee. A Honda motorcycle turns into a Kawasaki.
- *Impossible observation:* Elizabeth is talking to Marina by

telephone (voice only) and notices that Marina looks sad. Gaelan has unexplained knowledge of a scene in which he was not present, or a fact that the plot dictates he cannot possibly know.

- *Missing scene break:* Richard and Sonya are riding in a car in one paragraph, and in the next paragraph they are sitting on a couch in Lisa's living room. A paragraph is in Rosa's point of view, and the following paragraph jumps to Bernadine's point of view the next day in a different location. (These examples need either a few words of transition or a visual space break to indicate the change in location or point of view.)
- *Remembered dialogue or writing:* Headlines. Gravestones. Declarations. Letters. These are often shown and later recalled by characters, or repeated in narration. Yes, human memory is fallible; however, the author may have intended one version and forgotten to change the other, or they may consider it okay if the character remembers the wording a little differently. But the copyeditor's job is to ensure that any differences are deliberate.

All of these situations call for a query to the author explaining the problem and suggesting a solution if you can think of one.

Here are a few special types of action bloopers that may not be fixable at the copyediting stage, but you should still watch for them:

- *Chekhov's gun:* "If a gun appears in Act One, it should go off by Act Three." This principle, attributed to Russian playwright and author Anton Chekhov, is an admonishment to avoid loose ends. Elements that are introduced should be relevant to the story and not suggest a future action that never happens. These could be characters, objects, conversations, or situations that seem to foreshadow something but then go nowhere or disappear completely. Often these can be corrected by writing a query asking the author to either add some text to explain the presence of the element or revise the text to delete it. But such a change is up to the author.
- *"As you know, Bob . . .":* A cardinal rule of storycraft is "show, don't tell." Not following this rule often results in "info dumps"

not only in narration but also in dialogue, where characters tell each other things they already know about each other, just to inform the reader. "Remember last year, when you broke your leg skiing, and your brother Ramon had to drive down from his law office in Cheyenne to watch your two children?" This example is a little exaggerated but gives an idea of how awkward it sounds. Nobody talks like that! Ideally, "As you know, Bob" situations should have been fixed at an earlier editing stage; depending on the schedule, the copyediting stage is a bit late for most publishers to address it, but it still may be worth a direct query to the project manager. If you are working directly with the author, there's a better chance that you can explain the problem and ask for a revision to fix it.

Plot bloopers

Plot holes can vary from unlikely to impossible. Perhaps something could happen a certain way, but it would be so peculiar as to cause comment in real life—just as it might give readers pause. A wedding party could have seven bridesmaids and only a best man and no groomsmen, but that would be really odd, right? So unless a reason is given for this, a query is called for. Someone is driving from Paris to Munich, but somehow goes through Italy along the way. Why the detour? The FBI security expert simply swipes her phone screen to send an email. Why doesn't she use at least a passcode or biometric scan to keep it secure?

Most of the time these errors are the result of revisions or inadequate cross-checking of details to make sure they all make sense when taken as a whole. Keeping notes on seemingly insignificant details helps you notice when things don't line up as they should:

- In chapter 2, Natalie's parents live on the other side of the country. In chapter 23, Natalie and Blake go away for the weekend and drop the kids off at Natalie's parents' house. (That's a bit out of the way.)
- Finn lists the contents of their backpack for a hiking trip: shoes, pants, jacket, but no shirts? (Look for what's missing.)

- Jaya is shocked to see Varan at the coronation. But he is the empress's bodyguard and she had no reason to believe he wouldn't be there. (Why is she shocked?)
- Ingrid knows what Anthony whispered at his father's grave. But she was not at the funeral and he was standing alone when he said it, with no one nearby, and never told anyone what he said. (How could she know?)

Factual bloopers

Question everything. Even though a story is fictional, if it is set in the universe that we inhabit, it must be plausible. Sharpen your fact-checking skills: Do cannonballs explode? (Some do.) What kind of gun is a Glock 19? (It's a semiautomatic pistol, which means that its ammunition is contained in a magazine, not a cylinder.) In the 1981 Super Bowl, what was the score at halftime (and is Super Bowl one word or two)? (Raiders 20, Eagles 3; two words.) Is a Moskovitch a Bulgarian car? (Close; the *Moskvitch* is a Russian model that was manufactured in Bulgaria from 1966 to 1990.) What's the driving distance between Copenhagen and Berlin? (Nearly three hundred miles, and you'll have to take a ferry.)

Think about times when you've been pulled out of a story because some aspect of it was contrary to your specialized knowledge. A reader may have grown up in that city and know that the main thoroughfare runs east and west, not north and south. Another may work in that field or pursue that hobby and know that a process or object is described incorrectly. If you aren't familiar with a real object, person, place, organization, or topic, or if you think you know but aren't 100 percent sure, look it up or ask an expert. In fact, look it up or ask anyway. You may be surprised to learn what you thought you knew.

Anachronisms of both fact and language

Chapter 8 discussed anachronisms in dialogue, but they can also occur in narration, both as things that are out of place and as the words themselves. For example, a person cannot spend a loonie (dollar coin) in Canada in 1964, because the loonie wasn't minted until 1987; both the term and the object are anachronistic. In a story set in the twelfth century, "the hare rocketed across the field" should raise an eyebrow (and a query), because the concept of a rocket was unknown at that time. (*MW11* dates the noun to 1566 and the verb meaning "to attack with rockets" to 1794.)

Check the age of objects and concepts that are specific enough to have an origin date. *Dog* is generic enough for any period in history; *golden retriever* would be out of place before the mid-nineteenth century. Songs, books, and other things that have titles usually have a known release or publication date; check the accuracy of the title as well as whether it existed at the time of the story, or whether the character would know of it. A new song that was popular in England in 1820 may not have made it across the Atlantic by 1822. Put yourself in the story and question everything: Is this something that this character at this time would have eaten, worn, owned, used, looked like, traveled in, known, said, sung? Is this object or concept out of place?

Anachronisms can exist within the time range of the story as well. The regular NBA (basketball) season typically runs from October to April, so how can Raymond be watching the Knicks game on TV in August? Asparagus is a spring vegetable in the Northern Hemisphere, and although Mother Nature can be a mad scientist, picking fresh wild asparagus in October would be a strange thing. If a specific thing is described as happening at a certain time of the day, month, or year, question whether it makes sense in relation to the plot and look it up if there is any doubt.

Deliberate obfuscation and fictionalization

Although factual errors can creep in, sometimes "errors" are the author's deliberate choice. A big reason for this is privacy. Using real (or potentially real) phone numbers ("867-5309"), email addresses, street addresses, and other information that might belong to a real person can create headaches (and possibly litigation), thanks to pranksters and others. So the address for a fictional building in a real place might be at the corner of two streets that don't intersect, or in the middle of a lake—deliberately, so that no one can bother a real-life occupant. You can query such discrepancies when you find them, but bear in mind when writing your query that the discrepancy may be on purpose.

Look at characters' contact information. Does that email address look real? (Would you want your real email address to be attributed to a fictional character and published in a book? Most people probably would not.) One way around this is to invent a fictional domain: [name]@gmail.com is probably taken, whereas [name]@coolmail .com (not an active domain as I write this) is not. Another (but a more time-consuming) solution is for the author to reserve any email addresses on a real domain, to lock them out from being taken by someone else. A third option, if the email address isn't really needed in the story, is to simply mention it in passing instead of stating it outright (*She glanced at his email address at the top of the screen*). These are all options you can suggest in a query if you spot a potential problem. The same sort of logic applies for real-looking phone numbers, street addresses, and the like.

Real people and other entities

Including real people, organizations, events, creative works, and so on can be problematic. A fictional person in the cast of a real movie? Query. A real band performing at a fictional music festival? Query. A fictional murder is committed at a real theme park? Query. A real author who wrote a fictional book? Query. Not only is it contrary to fact, but the real person or organization behind the name may not appreciate the use of their name or the association with the story, even if it's positive. It's one thing to mention them (*I was obsessed with Harry Styles; a midnight showing of* The Last Jedi *downtown*), but putting words in their mouth or ascribing actions to them is a bad idea. As soon as they are woven into the plot, interacting with the characters, or given negative associations, this can create issues. Help the author avoid potential legal problems and suggest changing the real-life reference to a fictional one. You can also suggest that the author consult a media lawyer in their jurisdiction for advice.

Trademarks

Trademark holders are careful to protect their brand names, and traditional publishers generally would like to avoid even the hint of a potential lawsuit or a cease-and-desist letter. If a trademarked term is used as a lowercased generic term too often and the owner does not defend it by insisting on proper use, the trademark (and its commercial value) can be lost as it becomes a generic term in the general lexicon. Examples of former trademarks in the United States are *aspirin, escalator, mimeograph, touch-tone,* and *zipper;* conversely, trademarks that many people think of as generic but are still being defended by their owners include *Band-Aid, Frisbee, Realtor,* and *Xerox.* And some terms are trademarks in some countries but not in others; one example is *Hoover,* which is a trademarked vacuum cleaner brand in the United States but a generic noun and verb (*I spent the morning hoovering the hallways*) in the United Kingdom.

So navigating trademarks can be tricky! In general, characters can use a Kleenex, drink a Coke, drive a Ferrari, and go to McDonald's; mentioning brand names can add a sense of time and place and help connect the reader to the story. In accordance with *CMOS,* trademark "bugs" (™ and ®) can and should be omitted. *The Copyeditor's Handbook* includes a helpful and detailed discussion in chapter 6, "Capitalization and the Treatment of Names." The following is a brief overview of the technical aspects of copyediting trademarks in fiction.

CAPITALIZATION

Best practice is to capitalize known trademarks. *MW11* identifies trademarked terms, and a Google search (see what I did there?) often supplies the name of the trademark holder and a link to its website, which should confirm the correct spelling and capitalization and sometimes provides the preferred generic term and information on how the company is protecting its trademark. In particular:

- *Initial cap:* Trademarks with an initial cap can be kept as is (*Purell, Frisbee, Sharpie*).
- *Intercaps:* Intercaps include trademarks with an initial lowercase letter followed by a capped letter (*eBay, iPad*) and those with capital letters in the middle (*QuickBooks, PayPal*). These should also be rendered in their original form. If a lowercased trademark begins a sentence, suggest a revision; "EBay isn't letting me log in" just looks funny.

- *Lowercased:* Even if the trademark holder renders its mark in all lowercase letters (*adidas*), it's best to initial cap it in text (*Adidas*) to identify it as a trademark.
- *All caps:* It may be a *MINI Cooper* according to the manufacturer's ad copy, but it's perfectly fine for Janette to drive a *Mini Cooper*.

However, the other side of the coin is that although it's recommended, there is no legal requirement to cap trademarks in running text, and, especially in fiction, doing so can look awkward and overwhelming. At least one major US trade publisher's house style calls for lowercasing certain trademarks as nouns if the author has used them as such, and as verbs generally (*googled* is a common example). Your dictionary can also guide you; for example, *MW11* allows for lowercasing *google*, *photoshop*, and *xerox* as verbs.

Check punctuation and possessive forms as well; chain stores are especially tricky, as many used to be possessive but have dropped the apostrophe, while others were never possessive at all. Compare *Ralphs*, *Vons*, *Albertsons*, *Wegmans*, *Michaels*, and *Starbucks* with *Marshall Field's*, *Macy's*, and *Bloomingdale's*, to mention a few examples.

USAGE

Although trademark holders generally insist that in print, trademarks should be capitalized and used only as adjectives describing the generic term, no one in real life cuts their finger and asks for "a Band-Aid brand adhesive bandage." And so the same should be true in fiction. People Google things, they go Rollerblading, they make dinner in the Crock-Pot. But whether to keep and cap trademarks or "verb" them is often a style decision that we will discuss shortly.

Another concern is that some trademarks are used inaccurately. For example, *Styrofoam* is a brand of polystyrene used to make foam insulation products for the construction industry and floral and craft foam products. However, people commonly use *styrofoam* to refer to foodware such as take-out containers, coffee cups, and coolers, even though those products are made from a different kind of polystyrene. *Realtor* is a trademark owned by the National Association of Realtors, used only to refer to its members; all Realtors are real estate agents, but not all real estate agents are Realtors. Both *Styrofoam* and *Realtor* are listed as trademarks in *MW11*, and their owners are still defending them—a strong argument for capping them in text and suggesting alternatives when they are used incorrectly. For *Styrofoam*, you can suggest substituting *foam, take-out, to-go,* or *disposable,* or deleting the descriptor outright if doing so makes sense in context; *Realtor* easily becomes *real estate agent* or *agent.*

TRADEMARK OR GENERIC?

A large part of copyediting fiction is maintaining the way people talk and think, even (and especially) when it's not technically or mechanically "correct." Continuing with an example from the preceding section, most people think of *crockpot* as a synonym for the generic term *slow cooker,* even if the one they own is a Hamilton Beach.

What to do? One approach is to insist on capping trademarks or substituting a generic term; the other is to lowercase them if they have fallen into common generic use. Some publishers follow the dictionary: if it's listed as a trademark in *MW11,* it must be treated as one. Others keep a list of particular trademarks that may be lowercased. Your author might lowercase all trademarks unless they explicitly mean that particular brand. Pay attention to the treatment of trademarks for accuracy and consistency.

The following trademarks (both current and former) appear frequently in fiction; most are followed by potential generic substitutions.

Baggie/baggie
Dumpster/dumpster
Frisbee
Jacuzzi/hot tub/whirlpool
Jet Ski
Listserv/email discussion list
Magic Marker/marker
Onesie/onesie
Plexiglas/plexiglass
Popsicle/ice pop
Rollerblade/inline skates (or skating)
Sharpie/marker

Sheetrock/drywall
Windbreaker/windbreaker/jacket
Ziploc/ziplock bag/sandwich bag/plastic bag

REPRESENTATION

No matter whether you're capping or lowercasing trademarked terms, pay attention to how they are discussed. It's fine to say that someone was snacking on Tasty-Doodles (here, standing in for a real product) while they watched TV; however, saying that the Tasty-Doodles gave them food poisoning might attract attention from the Tasty-Doodles Inc. legal department. If a real company or product is being portrayed in a negative light, the best course of action is to suggest a fictional version instead—one that bears no resemblance to its counterpart in real life.

Permissions

As long as we're talking about intellectual property, let's talk about protecting copyright. Fiction authors often use text created by others as part of their storycraft. Permissions is an entire specialty in itself, and both *CMOS* and *The Copyeditor's Handbook* have sections with extensive information on the topic. Watch for quoted materials that may require permission to be used, insert a query to ask if permission is needed or has been obtained, and check the accuracy of quotes where possible. Unlike nonfiction, fiction does not generally cite long extracts from real-world publications. However, it does often feature the following types of quoted material.

EPIGRAPHS AND OTHER QUOTED MATERIAL

Brief epigraphs and other quoted passages generally fall under fair use if they are taken from a long-form work such as a book or a play. Check the accuracy of the epigraph or quote and its attribution against reliable sources, if possible. Check that all epigraphs and sources are styled consistently: Are sources preceded by an em dash? Is the source styled as "*Title*, Author Name" or "Author Name, *Title*"? And finally, epigraphs are generally not enclosed in quotation marks (unless the quoted material itself is enclosed in quotation marks in the original).

SONG LYRICS AND POETRY

It's fine for a manuscript to mention the names of artists such as songwriters, musical groups, and poets and the titles of their compositions; simply check artist names and titles of works for accuracy and add them to your style sheet. However, excerpts of song lyrics and poetry, no matter how brief, are generally out of bounds because of the brevity of the original. In theory, it might be possible to obtain permission from the copyright holder, but in reality it's going to be extremely difficult or expensive or both. In most cases it's just not going to happen. So, for example, if the main character's rock band is belting out a song, it's okay to mention the title or refer to the general theme of the song, but if lyrics are desired it's best that they write their own song.

Always query song lyrics or poetry that are not clearly the original work of the author. If the manuscript is being traditionally published, the publisher should have reviewed it for any materials that need permission and resolved those issues before the copyediting stage; if so, you may find credit or permission statements on the copyright page or in the acknowledgments, if you receive those materials along with the main manuscript. However, sometimes things slip through, and the copyeditor serves as another pair of eyes. And an indie author, in addition to not having a publisher watching out for this, may not be familiar with the permissions issues involved, so due diligence on the part of the copyeditor is even more important. Even if permission has apparently been obtained and credits are listed, a query asking for confirmation is a very good idea.

Conclusion

I hope that this book has given you some insight into the sorts of things that a skilled fiction copyeditor needs to be aware of, as well as techniques for keeping track of the myriad details that make up a story and create a believable world in which readers can immerse themselves. I leave you with these closing reminders:

Be flexible

Each fiction manuscript is a unique creation. Although some structure is needed and some rules are immutable, remember that a style guide is just a guide. Rules are made to be broken if doing so serves the story.

Use your Spidey-sense

Suspension of disbelief is a fragile thing; it can all fall apart if the smallest detail doesn't ring true. Even though the world of the story is made up, it still has to be internally consistent, whether within its own wholly invented universe or the one that we inhabit in reality—or a universe that's a combination of both. Keep your Spidey-sense tuned to catch those little glitches. Look things up if you're not sure; your reference sources include those in the real world as well as your notes on the style sheet you create based on the manuscript itself. Remember Twain: Truth is stranger than fiction, because fiction has to make sense.

Respect the author

The author has entrusted you with their creative work, and at the copyediting stage you are merely polishing the remaining rough edges. Let the author tell their story; it's not *your* book. Understand and respect the conventions of the genre and the author's deliberate choices. Query kindly, gently, and thoughtfully; make suggestions but do not dictate. Always remember that it's an honor to be invited into the creative process.

Serve the readers

Consider the audience: they may be the author's dedicated fan base, familiar with the world and its backstory and characters, or they may be first-time readers. Help them enjoy the pleasure of reading without getting hung up on mechanical glitches, biased language, or awkward details that pull them out of the story. Suspension of disbelief relies on consistency and flow.

Have fun!

Finally, have fun! Part of the pleasure of copyediting fiction is getting to enjoy the story along with the readers. You'll learn all sorts of interesting facts, discover new vocabulary, visit places you've never visited before (and some that exist only on the page), meet new people, and be amazed at the inventiveness of our authors who create such wonderful worlds and inspire us to think, feel, wonder, escape, imagine, love, laugh, cry, yearn, hope, and more. I think it's the best job in the world, and I hope you do too.

Acknowledgments

I've copyedited hundreds of acknowledgments sections, and now that it's time to write my own, it's easy to summon the immense gratitude that always comes through. A book is definitely not the sole output of one person, and *The Chicago Guide to Copyediting Fiction* would not have happened without the support of the people I thank here.

I would not have the experience on which to base this book if Lara M. Robbins had not taken a chance on me and hired me to copyedit fiction for Penguin a mere year after I started freelancing. She was my sole fiction client for many years, and she coached me, encouraged me, and sent me as many fiction copyediting projects as I wanted for nearly two decades, until she left Penguin literally for greener pastures. I am honored to call her my colleague and my friend. My thanks go also to the other publishers, project managers, and authors who entrust me with their wonderful manuscripts and ask me to copyedit their subsequent books.

Not every copyeditor aspires to be an author, but Erin Brenner and Jake Poinier both took the time to sit down with me early on and toss around ideas about what direction a book for editors about copyediting fiction might take. I am grateful for their specific advice and ideas. And at one conference, Geoff Hart repeatedly urged me to "Write the book! Write the book!" So I did. Thanks for your enthusiasm.

Executive editor Mary Laur at the University of Chicago Press has been a champion of this concept since I met her at the 2019 EFA conference in Chicago. I am told that Marilyn Schwartz, who was having lunch with her following my presentation, urged her, "You should get Amy to write a book," and Mary replied, "I'm way ahead of you." They didn't know that I had already started making notes for one. I had a wonderful conversation with Marilyn a month later at the Northwest Editors Guild conference in Seattle. I thank Marilyn for conspiring with Mary to help me get my book started. And I thank Mary for enthusiastically shepherding me, a newbie author, through the entire process.

Before you write a book, you write a proposal, a stage in which I was also a complete greenhorn. I am grateful to Mary Laur and to Karin Horler and Kristine Hunt for their guidance, suggestions, and encouragement, as well as to the anonymous peer reviewers for showing me how to take my rough outline to the next level.

I thank my fellow fiction copyeditors for answering a detailed questionnaire to give me insight into how other copyeditors work, so that I could provide broader coverage of ways to approach a fiction manuscript: Elizabeth Flynn, Joyce Grant, Katherine Kirk, Alice McVeigh, Tanis Nessler, Lori Paximadis, and Lara M. Robbins. Geoff Hart and Kia Thomas allowed me to use some of their writings as prompts to create examples; any illustrative errors are completely invented and not their creation!

Sarah Grey, Christine Ma, Lori Paximadis, Lara M. Robbins, Carol Saller, and Lisa S. Williams reviewed my penultimate draft and made many valuable corrections and suggestions. In particular, I thank Lori Paximadis, whose copyediting philosophy aligns so closely with mine that I think she must have the other half of this amulet, for many conversations, text and Zoom, in which she helped me separate the wheat from the chaff. Lori also generously provided a few illustrative examples to round out the content. Rachel Blackbirdsong, Christine Ma, and Crystal Shelley provided excellent feedback on the book's approach to authenticity and conscious language. Karin Cather reviewed the section on using real people and entities. Megan Krema made not one but two trips to my house to take photos in exchange for dog kisses.

I thank everyone at the University of Chicago Press who has supported and worked on *The Chicago Guide to Copyediting Fiction* and steered me through unfamiliar waters. Mary Laur and Mollie McFee guided me through the many organizational and technical details, and the anonymous reviewers helped me polish the manuscript one more time before final submission. I know firsthand how daunting it is to copyedit a book written by a copyeditor, but Erin DeWitt did a fabulous job of fixing the goobers that I could not see myself. Laura Poole followed up with her excellent proofreading skills. Janet Werner produced a marvelous index, just as I knew she would. Kudos to Rich Hendel for the engaging interior type design. I adore Kevin Quach's lively cover art, and I hope you do too.

The Chicago Guide to Copyediting Fiction could not have come to fruition without the steadfast mutual support of the Quad, my editorial mastermind group. These smart and amazing women have inspired and encouraged me to try so many new things and to accomplish more than I had ever imagined. Erin Brenner, Sarah Grey, Adrienne Montgomerie, Katharine O'Moore-Klopf, Lori Paximadis, and Laura Poole, you are my dearest friends and the sisters of my heart. I am grateful every single day for your presence in my life.

Finally, I thank my spouse, Boyd Featherston, for literally and figuratively keeping the home fires burning while I'm tucked away in my office. He wears many hats, among them housekeeper, chief cook and bottle washer, sommelier, facilities manager, head carpenter, groundskeeper, and dog wrangler. All I need to do is ask, and he provides. He has supported my aspirations ever since I took that first leap of faith into freelancing, and my business name includes part of his for good reason. Thank you, my love, for being my jester, my partner, my kindred spirit. My world is so much richer because you are in it.

Appendix A: Style Sheet Templates

Different publishers have different house style preferences. Indie authors each have their own preferences. You might follow different style conventions for different genres. Creating style sheet templates[1] for each client, type of client, or genre (or whatever organizing method suits you best) prepopulated with predetermined style choices makes the process of starting a project much easier. In this appendix, I will use the example of a style sheet template for each publisher client, because my fiction clients are all publishers, each with their own distinct house style, and that's what works for me. Once you have created a style sheet template, when you start a new project for an existing client you can simply open your style sheet template for that client; save a copy in the new project's folder with an appropriate name; fill in the author name, project title, project manager's name, due date, and whatever other administrative information you need to include; and away you go.

Let's say you want to create a style sheet template for your client Fruity Publishing Group (FPG). Start by opening a "blank" version of your usual style sheet. You probably include some standard elements on every style sheet: a header, such as "Style Sheet" and the date; the author's name and the book title; the project manager's name; your name; and sections labeled Numbers, Abbreviations, Punctuation, Typography, Usage, Miscellaneous, and an alphabetical word list. Some of these appear on every style sheet, but others such as names and dates will change.

Choose a way to indicate "reminder" elements (I use red font color; you might choose highlighting or some other method):

1. In this appendix, I use *template* in its generic sense—as an original blank document used as a starting point to create a new document for a specific purpose—rather than a Microsoft Word template (a document with a .dot, .dotx, or .dotm extension). I use a plain Word document (.docx) to create my style sheet "templates," strictly out of habit, but if you are comfortable creating and using Word templates for this purpose, go right ahead.

- Text to be filled in (such as the date, project author and title, and project manager's name). Use placeholder text to remind you to insert the correct information; for example, "00/00/2022" in place of the date, and "Author Name, *Book Title*" where that information will go).
- Style choices that differ from your usual habits (such as when an author requests "do not use the serial comma" with the publisher's approval, contrary to house style), to remind you to double-check those elements.
- Style options that have multiple valid choices. Include both options (for example, "cap/lowercase after a colon . . ."), and highlight them using your chosen method to remind you to indicate which one is being used and delete the one that is not (and to search for all instances as a double-check when possible).
- Reminders to yourself that will be deleted from the style sheet after the edit. For example, several imprints of my big publisher clients have requested that I not include my name on my style sheets for their projects, so I've added a reminder to myself to delete it (and the reminder list of imprint names) on my template (see figure A.1).

Next, add style elements from your style manual that you always put on your style sheet (here, let's assume *CMOS*): *use serial comma*; *spell out numbers through one hundred, large round numbers, and numbers in dialogue (exceptions follow)*; and so on.

Now add your client's style preferences from their style guide. Some of these may already be on your template if they agree with *CMOS*. Others may not be on your template, or they may be contrary to *CMOS*; if so, add them or overwrite the *CMOS* rule, as needed. Some preferences may need special "reminder" highlighting, as described in the preceding bulleted list, if they require a decision or differ from your usual practice. If your client has a list of preferred spellings for certain words, add those to your general word list. Add a note after each of these entries marking it as your client's style: [FPG style].

Finally, since not every style choice applies to every manuscript, you'll need to devise a way to mark style choices as final when you confirm them or add new ones. (This is only for your reference, as we'll see in a bit.) I use gray font color for all of the initial entries on my style sheet template (except for the "reminders" that I've flagged in red), and change the font color to black (using a macro) as I confirm or add entries. If it's black, it will be on the final style sheet. (You might choose a different method, such as adding or removing highlighting.) Red text for reminders remains red until the edit is complete.

When your style sheet template for each client is ready to use, it will look something like figure A.1. Headings and other elements that never change are in black; "boilerplate" entries that may or may not appear on the final style sheet are in gray (lighter gray tint in the figure); and entries that you'll need to change, decide on, pay special attention to, or delete are in red (darker gray tint in the figure). I have left the creation of the Characters, Places, and Timeline sections of the style sheet template as an exercise for the reader, depending on the format you choose. See part II.

When you start a new project for each client, open their style sheet template, save it with a new name in the project folder, and update it as you copyedit. When you're done, you can delete any remaining boilerplate (gray) entries, since they weren't used and didn't apply to this manuscript; review any remaining "reminder" (red or highlighted) entries and revise or delete them as needed; and change the entire document to black before returning it with the copyedited manuscript.

"This seems like a lot of work! Can't I just copy an old style sheet and use that?" That's a great idea for a subsequent book by the same author or the next book in a series (if you worked on the previous book), because it's already populated with the decisions from the last book and will help you maintain consistency. A style sheet template is most useful for a new stand-alone book or the first book for a new client. And the first time you forget to change something from a recycled style sheet, you'll wish you'd used a style sheet template that reminded you of what you need to update.

Even if you use the same style for every project, creating a style

(Apricot Press, Cranberry Books, Lychee Paperbacks, Quince Media, Tangelo House)
STYLE SHEET (00/00/2022)
Author Name, *Book Title*
REMOVE MY NAME FOR ABOVE IMPRINTS

Project Manager: Name   Copyeditor: Amy J. Schneider

References

Fruity Publishing Group House Style Guide (updated December 2021)
Chicago Manual of Style, 17th edition
Merriam-Webster's Collegiate Dictionary, 11th edition (online)

Numbers

generally, spell out: whole numbers through one hundred, large round numbers
centuries, decades, and ages

one-fifteen (time; FPG style)
1914–18 (FPG style)
October 11, 1996, . . .

Abbreviations

United States (n); US (a; no periods; FPG style)
United Kingdom (n); UK (a; no periods; FPG style)

St./Saint: see FPG style guide

ASAP   as soon as possible
DC   District of Columbia (FPG style)
L.A.   Los Angeles (FPG style)

Punctuation

punctuation following italicized words is always set italic:
period, comma, colon, semicolon (FPG style)

do not / use serial comma (follow AU, per FPG)
3-point ellipsis: always use 3-point Word ellipsis character, no spaces (FPG style)
4-point ellipsis: DO NOT USE (FPG style)
cap / lowercase after a colon if what follows is a complete sentence (follow AU, per FPG)

Harry Connick Jr. . . . (no comma; FPG style)

no interrobangs (use either ? or !) (FPG style)
allow occasional comma splices

's (possessives)

Sample Style Sheet Template, page 1 of 3

Figure A.1. Sample style sheet template. Text with a lighter gray tint behind it represents gray ("boilerplate") text; text with a darker gray tint represents red ("reminder") text.

sheet template saves you time and effort because you have your default style choices already in place. Review your style sheet templates periodically (yearly, and when you receive new versions of house style or a new edition of your style manual, such as *CMOS*) to be sure they're up-to-date.

Typography

cap prepositions of FIVE or more letters in headlines/titles (FPG style)
no ALL CAPS for emphasis; change to italic (FPG style)

direct thought, imagined/remembered/mouthed dialogue italic
words as words italic/roman with quotes (follow AU, per FPG)
signs in small caps: a for sale sign (FPG style)

in address: (lowercased terms here)
                Doctor, Officer (FPG style)

the Yangtze and Yellow Rivers (FPG style)
the corner of Main and Second Streets (FPG style)

Usage

maintain distinctions (except in dialogue):
        which/that, further/farther, while/although, since/because, between/among (FPG style)

OK to lowercase trademarks as verbs: googled, xeroxed, photoshopped

Most importantly, ... (FPG style)

Miscellaneous

follow AU for use of diacritics in spelling; add to word list (per FPG)

General Word List

Part of speech follows each word:

a	adjective	pa	predicate adjective
adv	adverb	pl n	plural noun
v	verb	prep	preposition
n	noun	interj	interjection
tm	trademark		

adviser (FPG style)
axe (FPG style)

backseat (FPG style)
blond (a, masc n; FPG style)
blonde (fem n; FPG style)

childcare (FPG style)
co-worker (FPG style)

daycare (FPG style)

email, ebook (FPG style)

fundraising, fundraiser (FPG style)

good night (FPG style)
goodbye (FPG style)

healthcare (n; FPG style)

internet, the net (FPG style)

mindset (FPG style)

offscreen, onscreen (FPG style)
offsite, onsite (FPG style)

seatbelt (FPG style)

townhouse (FPG style)
T-shirt, tee (FPG style)

voicemail (FPG style)

web, the (FPG style)
website (FPG style)

Sample Style Sheet Template, page 3 of 3

Appendix B: File Management

A well-organized file management and preparation system is a key element in working efficiently and maintaining version control. This appendix offers suggestions for how to develop a system for managing the various files you create as you copyedit.

Managing the manuscript

The first rule of file management is "Always stash the original file in a safe place." Don't leave the only copy in your email program or (heavens!) your download or temp folder; don't open the original file and work on it from start to finish. That's asking for disaster: an accidental deletion, a corrupted file, and—*poof!*—all your hard work is gone, and you have nothing to start over with.

Set up work folders for all of your clients in a system that works for you. Here's the system I use:

- A folder titled "Clients"
- Within the Clients folder, a folder for each client
- Within each client folder, a folder for each current project (titled with author surname and book title), plus an Archives folder for storing invoices, notes, and style sheets from completed projects

Within each project folder are at least three subfolders (named with a leading number to keep them in order):

1 ORIGINAL FILE: This is where I stash that precious original file exactly as it comes from the client. And I never ever make any changes to it. If the client sent a previous style sheet or a PDF of a previous book, those files go in this folder also.

2 WORKING FILES: This is where I save a *copy* of that original file to work on, and save new versions as I work. I save with a new name as I start editing each successive chapter (more on that in a bit); you might save a new version at the end of every hour or day or devise some other system. The important thing is to save the file with a new name regularly (whether by date, page or chapter number, or some other progress indicator; see the next section for ideas) and keep previous versions on file, in case a version gets corrupted, messed up, lost, or deleted; if disaster strikes, you can start with the most recent safe copy instead of from the beginning.

3 FINAL FILES: This folder contains the final edited manuscript, whether it consists of a single file (this is usually the case for publishers) or multiple files, such as the main manuscript plus front and back matter, reader's guide, and so on.

4 CLEANUP FILES (OPTIONAL): If I am doing cleanup (see chapter 2), this is where I put the files for that round, with another level of subfolders: **1** ORIGINAL CLEANUP FILES (for the edited files as they are sent to me for cleanup), **2** WORKING CLEANUP FILES (for files as I'm doing the cleanup), and **3** FINAL CLEANUP FILES (for the shiny perfect clean files ready for the compositor).

Along with these subfolders, the project folder also contains other files or notes the client sent, such as the client's transmittal letter or the PDF of a previous book (if provided); my style sheet; and my invoice.

Finally, when you finish a project, archive the style sheet along with your invoice and other project files that you created by moving the project file to your Archives folder. Most publishers ask the copyeditor to delete all versions of the manuscript file when the project is complete. However, having a copy of your own style sheet often comes in handy. (Occasionally a publisher calls me several months after I have completed an edit to ask if I still have the style sheet, because they can't find their copy. I produce it and I'm their hero!)

Version control

The preceding section covered the generalities of organizing different versions of the manuscript; now let's talk about the particulars of what's going on inside that "Working" folder. (This is an example of one possible system; feel free to create a system that makes sense for you.)

- *First pass:* The first version, the file on which I do my first light copyediting pass, is BookTitle reading.docx. (*.docx* is a

Microsoft Word file extension; if you're working in a different file format, the extension will also be different.)

- *Second pass:* When I start the second pass, the "big edit," I save a new copy of the manuscript file when beginning each chapter, giving it a new name that begins with the number of the chapter I'm working on: ch 01 BookTitle reading.docx, ch 02 BookTitle reading.docx, and so on. (Note the leading zero for chapters 1–9 to keep the versions in correct order in the folder list.)
- *Third pass:* When I do the third pass (really a bunch of mini-passes; see chapter 2), I save a single new copy named BookTitle 3rd pass.docx (the third pass usually doesn't take long, so I don't find it necessary to save multiple versions).
- *Final file:* After the third pass, I save the final file using the client's preferred naming format (if specified) or a generic but descriptive file name. For example:

Client-specified naming style:

ShortBookTitle_CE_02-24-2023

Generic naming style:

AuthorSurname-ShortBookTitle-CE-AJS-02-24-2023 (substitute your initials for "AJS")

Note the use of the editing stage (CE for *copyedited*) and the date. Avoid using terms like *FINAL* in file names (unless the client requires it); that can come back to bite you. I think we've all seen file names like BookTitle-NEW-FINAL-ver5-USE THIS ONE. I don't recommend going down that rabbit hole.

Managing the style sheet

When copyediting fiction, you'll have a few more main sections to deal with that are not part of a nonfiction style sheet. As you may recall from chapter 2, in addition to general style (with special sections devoted to elements of fiction), you will also need to record information about the following:

- Characters
- Places
- Timeline

You can keep all four main sections in one document, and use bookmarks to navigate quickly from one section to another; another method (the one I use) is to keep the style sheet as four separate documents, and switch from document to document as needed. Numbering them in order aids in navigation:

- 1 general style.docx
- 2 characters.docx
- 3 places.docx
- 4 timeline.docx

Numbering the file names this way means that in Microsoft Word (in this example, Word 2019), you can use the keyboard shortcut for your version of Word to Switch Windows (on the View tab), then press the number of the document to switch focus to it. (As long as your manuscript name begins with a letter, it will always be document 5 in the list.) No need to mouse to a window that may not be visible, or toggle among all of your open windows for all programs, which are in a different order each time depending on which one you were in last. After a while, these shortcuts become second nature. When the edit is complete, you can combine the separate documents into one style sheet for your client.

Appendix C: Multiple Monitors

With the advent of electronic copyediting, our screens became our workspaces and suddenly things got a lot more cramped. Manuscript, style sheet, dictionary, email and internet, and more, all vying for space on one screen. On a large monitor, you might be able to have two or three windows open side by side. But that's still a lot of flipping between windows to get to what you need.

However, it's a simple and game-changing upgrade to add monitors to your workspace. On a desktop computer, you can install a video card with multiple video ports. For a laptop, portable USB monitors fill the bill in your office or on the go. Add vertical (portrait) workspace to the mix by getting a desktop monitor that pivots or by turning your USB monitor ninety degrees. Your operating system software should enable you to manage multiple monitors and rotation settings; robust third-party software is also available.

How do I use all that space?

Figure C.1 shows the monitor arrangement I've had for many years. I use the monitors as follows:

- The leftmost widescreen monitor is my primary monitor; it's where my computer boots up. When I'm copyediting fiction, I keep the manuscript on the left side and my Characters and Places style sheets on the right side, one on top of the other (only one is visible at a time).[1]
- The two center portrait monitors are useful in nonfiction for copyediting long tables and paragraphs, seeing large sections of things like reference lists all at once, and proofreading full-page proofs. For fiction copyediting, I keep my general style sheet on the left one and my timeline on the right one. I refer to these documents most frequently, and it's convenient to see as much of them as possible. If I have a PDF of a previous

---

1. I recently replaced this 27-inch monitor with a 32-inch 4K monitor. Now I can fit *three* documents side by side on this display. Definitely a game-changer! Now I can have the manuscript, Characters, and Places all visible at once.

Figure C.1. Multiple monitors, desktop: two widescreen and two portrait (pivoting) monitors all connected to one tower. (Photo credit: Megan Krema)

book in the series for reference, that also goes on one of these monitors. (I also keep my Google Calendar here, because I can easily see an entire month at once with all activities visible, and my *MW11* dictionary window, so I can see as much of each word's entry as possible.)

- The rightmost widescreen monitor is reserved for the rest of my internet resources: email, browser, social media, and so on. It's off to the side so I can ignore it at will, but I can also copy a term into my browser and let it search while I return to the manuscript, and glance over once the search is complete. It's also convenient to keep several browser tabs open for reference: say, a map of the setting in the book, a biography of a historical subject, and the Amazon "Look Inside" page for a previous book in the series for searching.

Having the manuscript and three of my four style sheets visible all at once makes it easy to compare manuscript against the style sheet to check a style point, or to copy text from one to the other. I use keyboard shortcuts to navigate to the style sheet I need, and then bookmarks or a quick Find (if needed) to get to the correct section.

The mouse pointer can be hard to locate across several monitors.

Fortunately, your operating system has a solution. In Windows 10, the pointer options in the mouse settings allow you to show the location of the pointer when you press the CTRL key, which activates an animated "target" of concentric circles that zooms in on your pointer. Very handy! On Macs the mouse pointer locator is enabled by default. Simply wiggle your mouse (or your finger on the trackpad) quickly from left to right to temporarily embiggen the pointer. (If it's not enabled, check your mouse settings.)

Figure C.2 demonstrates the configuration I use with my laptop. Both external monitors (which can be used in landscape or portrait mode, but portrait works best in tight spaces) connect to the laptop via USB. When I'm away from home, suitcase space and public workspaces limit me to one external monitor, which I usually dedicate to vertical documents and email.

Other arrangements

You can add extra screen real estate in other ways: a laptop next to your desktop, or a tablet next to your laptop or desktop, for example.

Figure C.2. Multiple monitors, laptop: two portable USB monitors connected to a laptop. Each monitor can be rotated to widescreen. (Photo credit: Megan Krema)

But when you connect multiple monitors to one computer, you can copy and paste directly between windows and documents.

What's wrong with having just one monitor?

Nothing, really. Some people find multiple monitors overwhelming and prefer to use one ginormous monitor; others don't have the desk space. And if that setup works best for you, go for it! But multiple (ha!) studies suggest that adding a second monitor can increase efficiency by up to 50 percent, with diminishing returns up to about four monitors total. If the idea of multiple monitors intrigues you, try adding just one and see how you like it, and proceed from there.

Another advantage of multiple monitors is that if one dies, you have a spare or two so you can continue working until you can get a replacement.

I've read that it takes about two minutes after acquiring a second monitor to wonder why you didn't get one sooner. I thought so! And if you decide to explore the world of multiple monitors, I hope you do too.

Glossary

action beat: a narrative description of action that identifies the speaker but does not describe the dialogue; the action beat is a separate sentence from the dialogue

alliteration: repetition of the same sound at the beginning of several words in quick succession; see also *assonance* and *consonance*

assonance: repetition of similar sounds (usually vowels) in the middle of several words in quick succession; see also *alliteration* and *consonance*

character style: in Microsoft Word, a defined set of formatting rules that can be applied to text characters (such as bold or italic)

comment query: a query that is typed into the comment feature in a program such as Microsoft Word

consonance: repetition of similar sounds (usually consonants) in the middle of several words in quick succession; see also *alliteration* and *assonance*

copyediting: in fiction, the final stage of manuscript editing, in which the copyeditor conforms the text to a particular editorial style, considering spelling, grammar, punctuation, usage, and other elements; checks for accuracy and corrects or queries inconsistencies in plot, logic, and internal facts; creates a style sheet to record style choices and story facts; and queries unresolved issues, permissions needed, and anything else that requires further attention from the author

dialogue tag: a phrase such as *she said* that tells what was said and who said it, and perhaps how; the dialogue and the dialogue tag together form a complete sentence

direct thought: words that a character is actually thinking

echo: repetition, usually of whole words or parts of words, sometimes separated by a sentence or two

flagging: inserting queries (either as comments or directly in the text), highlighting repetitive issues, or writing a separate note to the author or publisher

garden-path sentence: a grammatically correct sentence that leads the reader to think the sentence is going one way ("down the garden path") when in fact it's going somewhere else, forcing the reader to backtrack to where the meaning went astray

global query: a query at the first instance of an issue, describing the general problem and asking the author to review it throughout the manuscript

head-hopping: an issue that occurs when the point of view changes or alternates quickly between two or more characters (seeing through their eyes, hearing their thoughts, feeling their feelings) without a scene break

house style: a publisher's internal style preferences, some of which may conform to *CMOS* and some of which may not

indirect thought: a description of what a character is thinking

inline query: a query that is inserted directly into the text of the manuscript, delimited by brackets, font attributes such as bold or highlight, and/or character style

narrative distance: the extent to which the reader is invited into the narrator's head and into the story

othering: treating someone or something as foreign, different, or separate

Oxford comma: see *serial comma*

paragraph style: in Microsoft Word, a defined set of formatting rules that can be applied to an entire paragraph

pass: one "trip" through a manuscript to perform a particular task (see *round*)

query: a question or explanation inserted in the manuscript, either as a comment or directly in the text; queries may be directed to the author, project manager, compositor, or designer

red herring: a false clue deliberately planted to mislead the reader

rhyme: assonance at the ends of words

round: a stage of editing that begins when the editor receives the manuscript and ends when the editor returns it to the client for review; a round usually consists of multiple passes (see *pass*)

scene break: a clearly delineated break or gap in the action

serial comma: the comma that precedes the final item in a list (*apples, oranges, and bananas*)

smothered verb: a verb that has been converted into a noun (*made a decision* instead of *decided*)

space break: white space in a manuscript that indicates a scene break; sometimes includes an ornament

style guide: generally, an internal document that lists a publisher's style preferences, particularly those that differ from a published style manual

style manual: generally, a published reference book that defines a particular editorial style; also called a *style guide*

style sheet: a document that records all of the style decisions for a particular manuscript

verb of utterance: a verb that describes the act of speaking

zombie rule: an outdated and sometimes incorrect grammar or usage rule that few language experts or editors observe

Recommended Resources

Style Manuals

The Australian Editing Handbook. 3rd rev. ed. Edited by Elizabeth Flann, Beryl Hill, and Lan Wang. Milton, Queensland: Wiley Australia, 2014.

The Canadian Press Stylebook: A Guide for Writing and Editing. 18th ed. Edited by James McCarten. Toronto: Canadian Press, 2018. Available in print or by subscription online at https://www.thecanadianpress.com/writing-guide/stylebook/.

The Canadian Style: A Guide to Writing and Editing. Rev. ed. Toronto: Dundurn Press, 1997.

The Chicago Manual of Style. 17th ed. Chicago: University of Chicago Press, 2017.

Editing Canadian English: A Guide for Editors, Writers, and Everyone Who Works with Words. 3rd ed. Toronto: Editors' Association of Canada, 2015.

New Oxford Style Manual. 3rd ed. Oxford: Oxford University Press, 2016. Combines *New Hart's Rules* and the *New Oxford Dictionary for Writers and Editors*.

General Dictionaries

American Heritage Dictionary of the English Language. 5th ed. Boston: Houghton Mifflin, 2016.

Australian Oxford Dictionary. 2nd ed. Oxford: Oxford University Press, 2005.

Canadian Oxford Dictionary. 2nd ed. Oxford: Oxford University Press, 2005.

Collins English Dictionary. 13th ed. Glasgow: HarperCollins, 2017.

Collins Free Online Dictionary. https://www.collinsdictionary.com/us/.

Merriam-Webster's Collegiate Dictionary. 11th ed. Springfield, MA: Merriam-Webster, 2003.

Merriam-Webster Unabridged. Available by subscription online at http://unabridged.merriam-webster.com/. Also provides access to the *Collegiate Dictionary* and the *Collegiate Thesaurus*.

Oxford English Dictionary. Available by subscription online at http://www.oed.com.

Language, Grammar, and Usage Resources

Ammer, Christine. *The American Heritage Dictionary of Idioms*. Boston: Houghton Mifflin Harcourt, 2013.

Barber, Katherine. *Only in Canada, You Say: A Treasury of Canadian Language*. Don Mills, ON: Oxford University Press, 2008.

Bartsch-Parker, Elizabeth, et al. *British Phrasebook.* Victoria, Australia: Lonely Planet, 1999.

Bernstein, Theodore. *The Careful Writer: A Modern Guide to English Usage.* 1965. Reprint, New York: Free Press, 1995.

Bernstein, Theodore. *Miss Thistlebottom's Hobgoblins: The Careful Writer's Guide to the Taboos, Bugbears, and Outmoded Rules of English Usage.* New York: Farrar, Straus and Giroux, 1971.

BuzzFeed Style Guide. https://www.buzzfeed.com/emmyf/buzzfeed-style -guide/.

Charles, KJ. "Enter Title Here" (blog post on nobility titles). https:// kjcharleswriter.com/2016/07/27/enter-title-here-2/.

Corpus of Contemporary American English (COCA). http://corpus.byu.edu/ coca/.

Corpus of Historical American English (COHA). http://corpus.byu.edu/coha/.

Dictionary of American Regional English. Available by subscription online at https://www.daredictionary.com/.

Garner, Bryan A. *The Chicago Guide to Grammar, Usage, and Punctuation.* Chicago: University of Chicago Press, 2016.

Garner, Bryan A. *Garner's Modern English Usage.* 4th ed. New York: Oxford University Press, 2016.

Google Books Ngram Viewer. https://books.google.com/ngrams/.

Google Trends. https://trends.google.com/.

Green's Dictionary of Slang. http://greensdictofslang.com/.

Historical Dictionary of Science Fiction. https://sfdictionary.com/.

Historical Thesaurus of English. https://ht.ac.uk/.

Johnson, Edward D. *The Handbook of Good English.* New York: Washington Square Press, 1991.

Spivak, Gael. "The Singular 'They' Is Gaining Acceptance." *Our Languages* (blog). Government of Canada, October 23, 2017. https://www.noslangues -ourlanguages.gc.ca/en/blogue-blog/singular-they-eng/.

Thomas, Kia. *A Very Sweary Dictionary.* Monee, IL: Kia Thomas, 2020.

Urban Dictionary. https://www.urbandictionary.com/.

Writing and Editing Resources

Bradburn, Richard. *Self-Editing for Self-Publishers: Incorporating: A Style Guide for Fiction.* Reen, 2020. Kindle.

Browne, Renni, and Dave King. *Self-Editing for Fiction Writers: How to Edit Yourself into Print.* 2nd ed. HarperCollins, 2004. Kindle.

Butcher, Judith, Caroline Drake, and Maureen Leach. *Butcher's Copy-Editing: The Cambridge Handbook for Editors, Copy-Editors and Proofreaders.* 4th ed. Cambridge: Cambridge University Press, 2006.

Douglas, Carla, and Corina Koch MacLeod. *You've Got Style: A Writer's Guide to Copyediting*. Don't Panic Books, 2015. Kindle.

Einsohn, Amy, and Marilyn Schwartz. *The Copyeditor's Handbook: A Guide for Book Publishing and Corporate Communications*. 4th ed. Oakland: University of California Press, 2019.

Harnby, Louise. *Editing Fiction at Sentence Level*. Louise Harnby, 2019. Kindle.

Hill, Beth. *The Magic of Fiction: Crafting Words into Story—The Writer's Guide to Writing and Editing*. 2nd ed. Atlanta: Title Page Books, 2016.

Judd, Karen. *Copyediting: A Practical Guide*. 3rd ed. Menlo Park, CA: Crisp, 2001.

McNees, Pat. Writers and Editors. https://www.writersandeditors.com/.

O'Moore-Klopf, Katharine. "Copyeditors' Knowledge Base." KOK Edit. http://www.kokedit.com/ckb.php.

Conscious Language Resources

Brown, Laura. "ASL: Writing a Visual Language." Disability in Kidlit, May 19, 2017. https://disabilityinkidlit.com/2017/05/19/asl-writing-a-visual-language/.

Conscious Style Guide. http://www.consciousstyleguide.com/.

The Diversity Style Guide. https://diversitystyleguide.com/.

GLAAD (Gay and Lesbian Alliance against Defamation). *Media Reference Guide*. 10th ed. October 2016. https://www.glaad.org/reference/.

Harnby, Louise. *Editing Fiction Containing Gender-Neutral Pronouns*. London: Chartered Institute of Editing and Proofreading, 2021.

Maggio, Rosalie. *Unspinning the Spin: The Women's Media Center Guide to Fair and Accurate Language*. Washington, DC: Women's Media Center, 2014.

Otmar, Renée. *Editing for Sensitivity, Diversity and Inclusion*. Victoria, Australia: Renée Otmar Consultancy, 2020.

Schwartz, Marilyn, et al. *Guidelines for Bias-Free Writing*. Bloomington: Indiana University Press, 1995.

Shelley, Crystal. "Resources" (especially "Conscious and Inclusive Language" and the Conscious Language Toolkit for Editors). *Rabbit with a Red Pen* (blog). https://www.rabbitwitharedpen.com/resources.

Wilkins, Ebonye Gussine. *Respectful Querying with Nuance*. New York: Editorial Freelancers Association, 2020.

Writing with Color. https://writingwithcolor.tumblr.com/.

Younging, Gregory. *Elements of Indigenous Style: A Guide for Writing by and about Indigenous Peoples*. Edmonton, AB: Brush Education, 2018.

General Books on Writing and Editing

Ginna, Peter, ed. *What Editors Do: The Art, Craft, and Business of Book Editing.* Chicago: University of Chicago Press, 2017.

McCullough, Gretchen. *Because Internet: Understanding How Language Is Changing.* New York: Riverhead Books, 2019.

Saller, Carol Fisher. *The Subversive Copyeditor: Advice from Chicago.* 2nd ed. Chicago: University of Chicago Press, 2016.

University of Chicago Press Editorial Staff. *But Can I Start a Sentence with "But"?* With a foreword by Carol Fisher Saller. Chicago: University of Chicago Press, 2016.

Walsh, Bill. *The Elephants of Style: A Trunkload of Tips on the Big Issues and Gray Areas of Contemporary American English.* New York: McGraw-Hill, 2004.

Walsh, Bill. *Lapsing into a Comma: A Curmudgeon's Guide to the Many Things That Can Go Wrong in Print—and How to Avoid Them.* New York: McGraw-Hill, 2000.

Walsh, Bill. *Yes, I Could Care Less: How to Be a Language Snob without Being a Jerk.* New York: St. Martin's Griffin, 2013.

Professional Organizations

ACES: The Society for Editing. https://aceseditors.org/.

Chartered Institute of Editing and Proofreading (CIEP). https://www.ciep .uk/.

Editorial Freelancers Association (EFA). https://www.the-efa.org/.

Editors Canada. https://www.editors.ca/.

Institute of Professional Editors Limited (IPEd). http://iped-editors.org/.

Editorial Training

New York University. http://www.nyu.edu/.

Simon Fraser University. https://www.sfu.ca/.

UC Berkeley Extension. https://extension.berkeley.edu/.

Toronto Metropolitan University, Chang School of Continuing Education. http://continuing.torontomu.ca/.

UC San Diego Extension. https://extension.ucsd.edu/.

University of Chicago Graham School. https://grahamschool.uchicago.edu/.

Technical Resources

Beverley, Paul. *Macros for Editors.* http://www.archivepub.co.uk/book.html. Microsoft Word ebook.

The Editorium (ETKPlus and other tools and resources). https://www .editorium.com/.

Horler, Karin. *Google Docs for Editors*. New York: Editorial Freelancers Association, 2018.

Intelligent Editing (PerfectIt). https://www.intelligentediting.com/.

Lyon, Jack. *Macro Cookbook for Microsoft Word*. West Valley City, UT: Editorium, 2012.

Lyon, Jack. *Wildcard Cookbook for Microsoft Word*. West Valley City, UT: Editorium, 2015.

Montgomerie, Adrienne. *Editing in Word 365*. Kingston, ON: Right Angels and Polo Bears, 2022.

Montgomerie, Adrienne. "PDF Markup Basics for Proofreaders & Copyeditors." *Right Angels and Polo Bears: Adventures in Editing* (blog). https://scieditor.ca/2019/02/pdf-markup-basics-for-proofreaders -copyeditors/.

Powers, Hilary. *Making Word 2010 Work for You: An Editorial Guide to the Tools of the Trade*. New York: Editorial Freelancers Association, 2014.

Online Resources to Follow

Brenner, Erin. *Right Touch Editing* (blog). http://righttouchediting.com/blog/.

CMOS Shop Talk (blog; particularly the "Fiction+" section). https://cmosshoptalk.com/.

Copyediting-L (email discussion list). http://www.copyediting-l.info/.

Fogarty, Mignon. *Grammar Girl* (blog). https://www.quickanddirtytips.com/grammar-girl/.

Harnby, Louise. Fiction Editor and Proofreader. https://louiseharnby proofreader.com/.

Hill, Beth. *The Editor's Blog*. http://theeditorsblog.net/.

Montgomerie, Adrienne. *Right Angels and Polo Bears: Adventures in Editing* (blog). https://scieditor.ca.

Owen, Jonathon. *Arrant Pedantry* (blog). https://www.arrantpedantry.com/.

"Style Q&A." *The Chicago Manual of Style Online*. https://www .chicagomanualofstyle.org/qanda/latest.html.

Index